NO MATTER HOW SPELLED there
is but one correct pronunciation of
"Mackinac", and that is "Mackinaw".

~~~~~~~~~

BOUNDARIES OF OLD MICHILI-
MACKINAC. "The country west of
Quebec, south to and along the Ohio
to the west boundary of Minnesota
and all that country which drains into
Lakes Superior and Huron."

Old Fort Mackinac
on the
Hill of History

HERALD-LEADER PRESS

MENOMINEE, MICHIGAN, U. S. A.

1938

Old Fort Mackinac

on the

Hill of History

By

ROGER ANDREWS

❖

FORT MICHILIMACKINAC

St. Ignace 1672
Mackinaw City . . 1712
Mackinac Island . 1780

"THE MOST HISTORIC SPOT IN MICHIGAN"

To my beloved wife
MARY

OLD FORT MACKINAC

(Photo by George Nelidoff.)

Acknowledgements

The writer of this book is grateful indeed for an opportunity to present as best he can a newspaper man's story of Old Fort Mackinac on the Hill of History at Mackinac Island, and its direct succession to the ancient forts at St. Ignace and Mackinaw City, Michigan. These three forts were for years called "Michilimackinac" and their history is progressively related in the records of those vibrant days beginning nearly three hundred years ago.

They all played a dramatic part in the development of the Old Northwest and in the stirring Colonial and 19th Century history of our country.

This book, gladly written as a free gift to the State of Michigan, is an all too feeble expression of gratitude by the writer for the privilege of serving so many years as a member of the honorary Mackinac Island State Park Commission of Michigan. He has found ample compensation in the opportunity for research and study of Mackinac Island, Mackinaw City and St. Ignace which the preparation of this book afforded.

He earnestly hopes it will broaden the field of knowledge of the historic Straits of Mackinac country, and encourage the study of its heroic past.

Its publication has been financed from the tourist and travel funds of the State of Michigan, with hearty approval of the State Administrative Board and the Mackinac Island State Park Commission,

and all the receipts from its sale will go directly
back to the State Treasury of Michigan. The copyright has been freely assigned to the Mackinac
Island State Park Commission.

An earnest effort has been made to discover so
far as possible from fragmentary records available
the correct dates and names required for an accur-
ate story of those days of long ago.

Grateful, sincere acknowledgement is made of
the opportunity to quote herein from the histories
already printed of Mackinac, all of them written
long ago and today out of print. They are:

*   *   *

HISTORIC MACKINAC, written and published in
1918 (two volumes) by the Hon. Edwin O.
Wood, LLD., of Michigan, earnest and pains-
taking student of the history of the Northwest;
former president of both the Michigan State
Historical Commission and the Mackinac Island
State Park Commission. From the presses of
the MacMillan Company, New York City.
(Now out of print.) By permission of the
MacMillan Company.

MACKINAC, f o r m e r l y MICHILIMACKINAC,
written and published in 1895-6-7 by that eminent citizen, physician and soldier of Mackinac
Island, Brevet Lieutenant Colonel John R.
Bailey, M. D., whose record of nearly 50 years
service at Fort Mackinac and on the battle
fields of the Civil War will ever be cherished as

an example of devotion to duty and love of country. (Now out of print).

ANNALS OF FORT MACKINAC, written and published in 1883 by Lieut. Dwight H. Kelton, U. S. Army, who served with distinction as an officer at Fort Mackinac, and is buried at Arlington Cemetery, Washington, D. C. (Now out of print).

EARLY MACKINAC, written and published by the Rev. Meade C. Williams in 1901, for many years a trustee of the Old Mission Church on Mackinac Island, an ardent student of Mackinac history and beloved by all those whose privilege it was to know him. (Now out of print).

OLD MACKINAW, The Fortress of the Lakes, written and published in 1860 by W. P. Strickland, an earnest and indefatigable student of the early history of Mackinaw City. (Now out of print).

With gratitude, also, to all those authorities and students whose findings have been quoted or relied upon in the bibliography listed above, important contributors to the treasure house of our history.

The Author.

MACKINAC ISLAND.
July 1st, 1938.

Foreword

The vibrant drama of early North American history, prior to the events which produced the United States of America, contains no more inspiring and compelling chapters than those which hold the story of the Michilimackinac country.

In this more or less indefinitely bounded outpost of the old Northwest territory took place contests for possession, struggles for Indian fur trade, conspiracies of conquest, martyrdom for religion, fierce battles on land and lakes, and the alternate authority of three nations, whose flags rose and fell in the theater of war.

Onto this historic stage Jesuit fathers brought the message of Christianity, many of them to die at the stake or under the cruel tortures of the savage Indians; here the original sailing vessel on the Great Lakes made her first call and soon after found an unknown watery grave; here the immortal Father Jacques Marquette gave battle to ignorance and the anti-Christ, began his trip of discovery of the Mississippi river, suffered an early death on the wild shores of Lake Michigan, and was borne to his grave at St. Ignace by the longest cortege of Indian canoes ever assembled on any waters; here the redoubtable chief, Pontiac, when refused the uniform and dignity of a general's rank in the British army, planned the revengeful and bloody conspiracy which rocked the northwest and brought the cruel

massacre at what is now Mackinaw City, Michigan;
here was organized and operated the first corporation in America which gave John Jacob Astor control of the early American fur trade; here a Mormon
leader of 3,000 pilgrims established a kingdom,
assumed a crown and died a violent death.

Here Major Robert Rogers, hero of the best
selling book, "Northwest Passage", while commanding the British Fort Michilimackinac, planned
a conspiracy which would have sold the territory to
the defeated French and the distant Spaniards, but
ended with Rogers in a London prison; here the
Indian Chief, Wawassom (whose name, which
means "lightning" or "distant fire flashes", has in-
correctly gone into nearly all histories as Wawatam), saved the British fur trader, Alexander
Henry, his "blood brother", from death at an Indian stake; here took place the alternating territorial possession of Great Britain and the United
States, both by the violence of arms and the terms
of treaty; and here occurred the last events of the
war of the American Revolution and first engagement of the war of 1812.

The foregoing is but a fragmentary sketch of
the index of stirring events of past centuries in the
Michilimackinac country. As the "Northwest" territory of long ago its boundaries may well be defined
by simple use of its name. It covered an unlimited
and uncharted wilderness north and west of the
early discoveries and settlements along the Atlantic
Coast, from Canada to the Virginia colonies.

The author has not attempted in this book to do

more than record as best he can the history of the
Old Forts, all under the name of Michilimackinac,
with three closely linked locations, and which were
the defenses of early northwest development under
the flags of France, Great Britain and the United
States.   Around this twice-moved fort is woven a
story of historic adventure which deserves a permanent and prominent place in the archives of our
country.

THE FIRST
FORT MICHILIMACKINAC
At St. Ignace

CHAPTER ONE

The first authentic mention of defense and fortifications in the ancient Straits of Michilimackinac section tells us that in 1672 the Huron Indians built a "fortified village" on East Moran bay, at or very near the present site of the City of St. Ignace in the Upper Peninsula of Michigan.

In 1671, under instructions of the Intendant of Canada, Jean Talon, a company of French soldiers and priests, led by Daumont de St. Lusson, with a host of Indians, had gathered at Sault Ste. Marie and, formally raising the flag of France, taken possession "in the name of the Most High, Mighty and Redoubtable Monarch, Louis, Fourteenth of that name, Most Christian King of France, of all lands, both those which have been discovered and those which may be discovered hereafter, in all their length and breadth, bounded on the one side by the seas of the North and of the West, and on the other by the South Sea." Thousands of Indians, summoned from tribes far and wide, watched with awe this impressive and dramatic ceremony, "astonished to hear that there was any man on earth so great, rich and powerful."

In the autumn of 1672 a great war party of northern Indians, under the general leadership of the Ottawas of Manitoulin, on the war path against the powerful Sioux tribe located further south and west, suffered a disastrous defeat in what is now

northern Wisconsin. Banded with the Ottawas
were the warriors of the Huron tribe, the Pottawa-
tomies, and Sacs and Foxes. But in the St. Croix
valley, where the issues of battle were drawn, the
attacking expedition met an enemy who drove them
to rout and retreat. The invaders fled back north
in a winter marked by severe weather and unspeak-
able suffering. Those who died became a cannibal
food supply for the survivors, and none would
have returned alive had it not been for the bravery
of the Hurons who covered the rear of the war
party's retreat.

The remnant of the Hurons, on reaching St.
Ignace, established a village and constructed their
log fort in the same vicinity where the Jesuit missionaries, Fathers Dablon and Marquette, had some
two years before erected a crude chapel and found-
ed the mission of St. Ignatius.

Although this book is addressed to the military
and defense features of the three famous colonial
forts, and the protection of this Straits section suc-
cessively by means of primitive stockades and defenses at St. Ignace, Mackinaw City and Mackinac
Island, we pause to present in a few words a tribute
to that saintly and famous Jesuit priest, Father
Jacques Marquette. "Of gentle lineage, devoted to
his calling, and esteeming his life as nothing if it
might be sacrificed in the saving of souls, he was
also a scholar and scientist imbued with the spirit of
discovery."

Born at Laon, France, on June 1st, 1637, and
rigorously trained for his life work in the Jesuit college at Nancy, he reached Quebec in 1666 and four

An artist's conception of the landing of Nicolet on Mackinac Island, in June, 1634. This first white man to enter the Northwest Territory believed he had arrived at China, and disembarked in the robes of a Chinese mandarin. His salute with two ancient pistols scattered the Indian reception committee in quick order.

or five years later (the date being in some dispute) arrived, probably with, or just following, Father Claude Dablon, in the Michilimackinac section. There is a conflict of authorities regarding the point at which the first mission was established, with some controversial evidence from Jesuit history that it was on Mackinac Island. Be that as it may, the real scene of Marquette's labor was at St. Ignace, on the northern side of the Straits, where he established on what was known as Point Iroquois the historic Mission of St. Ignatius. From this base for two years the devoted priest ministered to the Indians, winning their hearts and earning their full confidence.

In 1672 he was joined by the explorer-priest, Louis Joliet, and they were given permission by their superiors to undertake an exploration of the "great waters" in the west, of which they had learned a little from the Indians. Their frail canoe departed from St. Ignace on May 17, 1673, and one month later, to a day, they discovered the upper waters of the Mississippi river. Marquette spent the next two years in mission work in what is now Illinois and Wisconsin, but his health was failing, and early in the spring of 1675 he started the return trip to his beloved St. Ignace. His condition rapidly grew worse, and he directed his Indians to make a landing at a point not far from the present city of Ludington, Michigan, where the great priest and discoverer passed away on May 18th, 1675.

For two years his body lay in the shallow grave, but, from the eloquent pen of Lieut. Col. John R. Bailey, famous surgeon and soldier of early Mackinac Island, we learn that "God did not suffer the remains of Marquette to be forgotten. On the second anniversary of his death the Algonquin Indians, together with a number from other tribes, repaired to the spot, disinterred the body and tenderly placed the remains in a neat box of birch bark, and conveyed them to St. Ignace. The sorrowing convoy consisted of thirty canoes in solemn single file procession. Following the rites of the church to which his life had been dedicated, interment was made in a little vault underneath the mission chapel."

With the later abandonment of St. Ignace by the Jesuits the location of the grave of Marquette was lost, but in 1877, Father Edward Jacker, the local priest, in company with David Murray, discovered the spot, and found the indisputable proof of its genuineness. Some of the bones were removed to a crypt in the halls of Marquette University at Milwaukee, but over the remaining relics a monument in his honor was erected at St. Ignace, and is today a veritable shrine for people of every creed, pausing there a moment to pay tribute to a martyr to his faith, and a courageous pioneer whose fame and name will ever endure.

The missionaries had come in a spirit of peace and religion, and for several years gave little thought to defense. When they built their first permanent church at St. Ignace in 1674, together with their combined mission house and residence, it was located close to the fortified Huron village, with but some crude stockade protection against the hostilities of neighboring Indians, who had proved to be unfriendly.

We may well imagine the awe with which the Indians at the St. Ignace mission and villages watched the approach in the harbor of the ship, Griffin, first sailing vessel on the Great Lakes, which came to anchor off St. Ignace on August 27, 1679, under command of that intrepid explorer and trader, Rene Robert Cavelier, sieur de la Salle. "The Griffin fired her cannon, and the Indians yelped in wonder and fright". The Red warriors surrounded the "great wooden canoe" with their frail birch bark craft, and gingerly surveyed at a safe distance the thunderous cannon.

Later in 1679 the Griffin, La Salle not being aboard, sailed from Green Bay for Niagara with a great load of furs, and was never again heard from. It is believed to have been lost either in the vicinity of the Straits of Mackinac or in Canada's Georgian bay. Commander Eugene F. McDonald, Jr., a noted Chicago naval reserve officer and yachtsman, has taken divers to a spot in the Georgian bay section where he believes traces of the wreck of the Griffin have been found, and will this year continue the search. La Salle later discovered the mouth of the Mississippi river. In 1687, on a subsequent expedition, he was murdered by his followers.

CHAPTER TWO

Between 1678 and 1681 it became apparent to the French government authorities at Montreal that great possibilities of profit existed in the increasing fur trade with the Indians of the northwest centering in the struggling settlement at St. Ignace, and a military detail of French soldiers was sent to occupy Fort St. Ignace (believed then to be named Fort DuBuade) under command of M. de Villeraye, the first listed French officer in the available records of two and one half centuries ago. Thus were the tricolors of France raised on the Straits of Michilimackinac. De Villeraye remained in charge of Fort St. Ignace until 1684, when he was relieved by M. de la Durantaye, who appears to have been the first officer designated as "commander of Michilimackinac", and having in his charge not only the meagre fortifications but the supervision of the fur trade and the "coureurs de bois that trade upon the lakes and the southern countries of Canada."

Commandant La Durantaye had plenty to do, for the hostile Iroquois were on the war path in other parts of the French possessions, with an eye towards acquiring Michilimackinac. St. Ignace had been made the military center of the Northwest, with the commandant invested with full authority over all the French in the Michilimackinac section.

The Iroquois, whose country was further east, were in more or less close alliance with the British

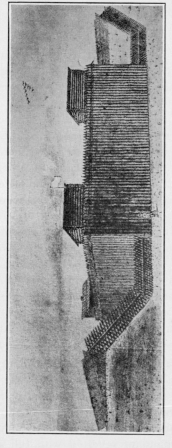

Original French design of Fort Michilimackinac at St. Ignace, 1762.
(From a copyright drawing by the late Arthur Lagron of Peoria, Illinois,
former engineer in the French army).

interests, both commercial and military, which looked with covetous eyes on the increasing value and importance of the northwest French fur trade. The sabotage of war was used by the British to rupture and destroy the friendship and co-operation which existed between the Indians and the French pioneers. In 1684, Sieur Daniel de Greysolon DuLhut (Duluth), referred to as "the king of the coureurs de bois" and who had commanded for a short time Fort St. Ignace, joined Nicolas Perrot in enlisting with La Durantaye in an expedition against the distant Iroquois, leaving an officer named Valtrie in command at Michilimackinac.

Near Niagara the French and Indian forces scored a decisive victory over the Iroquois, so that La Durantaye was able to return to Michilimackinac in triumph, hoping that the confidence of his Indian neighbors would be restored as to the potent power of the French king. There is little doubt that, had the Iroquois been victorious, the wavering northern tribes would have deserted to the English, after a massacre of all the French in the Michilimackinac region.

Returning to St. Ignace, the commandant, Durantaye and his able linguist, Nicolas Perrot (many of whose descendants now live on Mackinac Island), addressed themselves to the task of regaining the friendship of the Indians who had been weaned away by English advances. They met with only indifferent success, and probably the day was saved for the King of France by the arrival at St. Ignace, in 1690, of the new commander, Louvigny, with additional soldiers for garrison duty.

A French army officer at St. Ignace, at about this period, wrote as follows: "Opposite the Island (Mackinac) is a large anse (St. Ignace) on the north shore of the lake, in the middle of which area the French fort stands. Here there is a garrison and commander in chief of the district, who has under him the commanders of the various (Michilimackinac) posts. Both he and they are selected by the Governor-General of New France. This post is called Fort De Baude.

"The Jesuits' monastery, the French village and the village of the Huron Indians and the Outaouas (Ottawas) are adjacent to one another.

"It is well to observe that, in this country, the word 'town' is unknown; so that, if they wish to speak of Paris, they would describe it by the name 'the great village'.

"The position of this post is most advantageous, because it is quite close to Lake Huron, through which all the tribes of the south are obliged to pass when they go down to Montreal, and in coming back. None of them can pass without being observed, for the horizon is so clear that canoes can be seen from the fort at as great a distance as the keenest eye can reach."

Fort St. Ignace was described at this time as "made of stakes. Those in the outside row are thick as a man's thigh and about thirty feet high. The second row, inside, is quite a foot from the first, which is bent over onto it, and is to support and prop it up. The third row is four feet from the second and consists of stakes three and one half feet in diameter standing fifteen or sixteen feet out

of the ground. Now in that third row they have no
space at all between the stakes; on the contrary,
they set them as close together as they can, making
loop holes at intervals. As to the first two rows,
there is a space of about six inches between the
stakes, and thus the first and second rows do not
prevent them from seeing the enemy; there are no
bastions, and the fort is, strictly speaking, only an
enclosure."

But an inside enemy was at work towards the
destruction of this French outpost, in the form of
traffic in brandy, or "fire water", between the
French garrison, as well as the traders, and the
Indians. It was charged that "the commandant, his
officers and his soldiers have become traders with
the Indians, the principal article of their traffic
being eau de vie, dealt in at first secretly, but later
on openly and in cabarets."

The missionaries protested in vain to Frontenac,
the governor, but had some temporary success in
appealing to the French Court. For a time the traffic was curtailed, but the Indians were greatly in-
censed there-by and turned against the protesting
Jesuits. In 1694 relations had become so strained
and threats so alarming that Durantaye was relieved
from duty and succeeded by Antoine de la Mothe
—Cadillac. The studious historian, Parkman,
gives us this picture of the new commander: "Cadillac was amply gifted with the kind of intelligence
that consists of quick observation, sharpened by an
inveterate spirit of sarcasm; enterprising, energetic
and a bold and visionary schemer, with a restless
spirit, a nimble and biting wit, a Gascon impetuosity

of temperament, and as much devotion as an officer
of the King was forced to possess, coupled with
small love of priests and aversion to Jesuits."

Cadillac promptly advised his superior, Frontenac, of the growing hostility of the Indians at St.
Ignace, and of the danger that, were not brandy restored to them by the French, they would seek and
obtain it from the troublesome and competing English.   The controversy waged and increased between the priests and the forces of Cadillac, consisting of two hundred officers and men.

The Jesuit point of view was clearly set forth in
a letter written in St. Ignace by Father Stephen de
Carheil, "himself of noble blood, a veteran of the
Iroquois missions and one of the holiest of the
Jesuit priests", superior of the Ottawa missions, to
de la Carrieres, then governor general of New
France.   He had been in frontier mission work for
16 years, and was well informed on the St. Ignace
situation.   He wrote: "The missions are reduced to
such extremities that we can no longer maintain
them against an infinite multitude of evil acts of
brutality and violence, injustice and impiety, lewd
and shameless conduct.   To such acts the infamous
and baleful trade in brandy gives rise everywhere
without restraint.   In our despair there is no other
step to take than to leave our missions and abandon
them to the brandy traders, so that they may establish their trade of drunkenness and immorality."

This militant priest, believing that permission
to renew the brandy trade had been obtained from
the King of France by a false pretext, added that
"the soldiers do no real service to the King, for, in

Typical picture of early forts at St. Ignace, Mackinaw City and Sault Ste. Marie.
(From an old drawing).

reality, the commandants come here solely for the purpose of trading, in concert with their soldiers, without troubling themselves about anything else." He urged the Crown to discontinue the garrison and begged for "justice against the calumnies and violence of Monsieur de la Motte (Cadillac)."

CHAPTER THREE

In 1701, following seven strenuous years of bickering at St. Ignace, Cadillac was transferred to command the fort and settlement at Detroit. From the prolific pen of Richard R. Elliott, acknowledged authority on Indian and mission affairs, we learn that "the memories of his experience at St. Ignace (which included his administration of the entire Michilimackinac section) rankled in the soul of Cadillac, and when appointed commandant at Detroit he conceived the design of depopulating Michilimackinac (St. Ignace) by inducing the Ottawa and Huron Indians to leave the Straits, and come down and build homes in the vicinity of Detroit". This plan Cadillac recommended to the Court of France as an effective way to centralize the Indians of the west, to maintain with them a potent organization against the hostile Iroquois and to place the rapidly increasing fur trade more than ever under French control and away from the aggressions of the English. Several thousand Indians followed Cadillac to Detroit, and in despair the Jesuits burned their St. Ignace mission buildings and sorrowfully returned to Montreal in 1705.

The abandonment of this strategically located fort and post at St. Ignace was a source of great embarrassment to the governor general of Canada, and somewhere between 1706 and 1708 he persuaded Father Marest to return to St. Ignace,

promising to promptly send to him the former commandant, Louvigny, and a military company.
Father Marest reported as follows: "The savages
declare that they are now convinced that their
French Father (the King) would not abandon
them; that whatever happened in Detroit, the
French would always be secure here." The neces-
sity of re-establishing the St. Ignace post is covered
in the report made by M.d'Aigrement in 1708 advising that "if the post (fort) at Michilimackinac
were given up entirely and all the Ottawas to go
from there and settle in Detroit, the greater part of
the beaver skins would go to the English, by the
agency of the Iroquois. A garrison post at the
Straits is necessary, from which to go and bring
these furs in." He concluded that "Michilimackinac
is the most advantageous post in Canada."

The quarrelsome and sharp tongued Cadillac,
at Detroit, took exception to the requests that the
St. Ignace post and activities be revived, and in the
same year in which the restoration was promised to
Father Marest by the Canadian Governor General,
Cadillac issued a statement saying: "This proposed
re-establishment of the post at Michilimackinac (St.
Ignace) has great allurements for the Governor-
General because it makes him master of the commerce. If Michilimackinac were abandoned the
savages would no longer resort to Montreal, and
consequently the Governor-General would no longer receive his annual presents from them."

Regardless of the critics, the Governor-General
sent Father Marest on his trip of restoration, promising Louvigny would at once follow. This officer

was endorsed as a man "much respected and loved by the savages" and "an intelligent and vigilant officer". He has previously commanded Fort St. Ignace from 1690 to 1694. Added to these re-commendations was the statement: "If His Majesty (the King of France) adheres to the intention of having this post (Fort St. Ignace) re-established it will be essential, in order to make the Indians understand that it is a permanent one, to have a fort and some houses built there, as there used to be before, and twenty soldiers and a sergeant will be required for building this fort and keeping it up".

After his return north Father Marest wrote to Montreal: "If the savages ever wished for Monsieur de Louvigny it is now, and they say it is absolutely necessary for him to come for the safety of the country, to reconcile them with one another, to keep together those whom the war has already brought back to Michilimackinac. The Chief Koutaouiliboe said to me: 'Our Father Onontio (the French king) promised to send us Monsieur de Louvigny, and now he wants to deceive us this year as he has done all other years. He tells us that he loves his children, the savages of Michilimackinac, above all, yet he seems to abandon them entirely. Formerly, before Detroit was established, we who had settled at Michilimackinac were people of im-portance. If our Father loves us why does he not think of establishing again this place for us and of sending us the man he has promised for such a long time, to give spirit to those who have none, to strengthen us against our enemies if they attack us,

Death of Father Marquette, 1675.

and to prevent us from scattering now that we have come together again."

There must have also been plenty of government red tape in those remote days, for although Father Marest came back to St. Ignace in 1708, the promised military contingent did not arrive at the Straits until about 1712, if indeed they then or later re-established the fort and trading posts at St. Ignace. Charlevoix, journeying to St. Ignace in 1721, says in his journal: "I arrived the 28th at this post (St. Ignace) which is much fallen into decay since M. de la Motte Cadillac carried to the Narrows (Detroit) most of the Indians who were settled here."

There is a sharp conflict of historians as to the exact date on which the French moved their military and fur trade operations from St. Ignace, on the north side, to the present Mackinaw City, on the south side of the Straits of Mackinac. The blanket name of Michilimackinac for the entire region befogs the issue and leaves the record in doubt.

Somewhere between 1706 and 1724, according to a sort of consensus of historical opinion, the French established themselves at Mackinaw City, built a fort and trading post and gave up their headquarters at St. Ignace. Perhaps it was really in 1712 or a little later when M. Louvigny finally was dispatched to the north country, with his soldiers, and at that time found a new location at Mackinaw City, the northern point of what is now the lower peninsula of Michigan.

To St. Ignace belongs the credit for being chosen as the first of these French colonial outposts, and it is only to be regretted that history gives us no greater detail of the dramatic events of its vibrant story.

Through the efforts of United States Senator Prentiss M. Brown, a distinguished citizen of St. Ignace, where he was born, a Federal Works Progress Administration appropriation was obtained early in 1938 for the reconstruction of old Fort St. Ignace (Fort DuBuade) along its original lines on a high palisade just east of the city of St. Ignace, to be completed in the following early summer. This splendid plan will provide the Straits of Mackinac with the three ancient forts around which this book is written; viz, the original Fort Mackinac on Mackinac Island, and the reconstructed forts, exact duplicates of their originals, at St. Ignace on the north shore and Mackinaw City (Fort Michilimackinac) on the south shore.

The historical traditions of St. Ignace owe much of their preservation to the earnest research and devotion of the Reverend Father John T. Holland, whose life and service reflect the spirit which characterized his Jesuit predecessors of the Seventeenth century. This patriotic priest has made an analytical study of many books, documents and maps relating to the history of St. Ignace, both clerical and secular, and presented the government authorities with maps and drawings upon which are based the reconstruction of the old fort. Father Holland's ambition is to see an adequate monument erected at St. Ignace in memory of Father Marquette.

The annual host of summer visitors to St. Ignace, of every faith and from every state in the

Union, include the grave of Pere Marquette in their "must" list of places to see and honor. Above it once stood the ancient Jesuit mission church. Time and fire destroyed or brought into disuse later church buildings at St. Ignace, and Catholics now worship in a modern brick edifice on high ground, overlooking the beautiful harbor. This St. Ignatius church is also a travel Mecca, for on its vestry wall hangs one of the oldest historical pictures in the country, an oil painting of St. Ignatius Loyola, believed to have been brought to St. Ignace by Father Marquette in 1671. It adorned the old Mission church until the latter was destroyed by fire in 1700. Cadillac took the revered picture with him to Detroit in 1701 where it remained until 1835.

The sainted priest, Ignatius Loyola, commander in chief of the army of Spain in 1521, was severely wounded in battle, and made a vow that should he recover he would devote his life to God. He was the founder of the historic Society of Jesus, the famed order of the Jesuits. The ancient painting may be freely viewed by visitors at the St. Ignace church.

FRENCH COMMANDANTS OF ANCIENT
FORTS IN ST. IGNACE AND
MACKINAW CITY

(Note—the following names are all that appear in the old official records which this author has been able to uncover).

ST. IGNACE

1681—M. de Villaye.

1683—M. de la Durantaye.

1684—Daniel de Greysolon De Lhut.

1687—M. de la Durantaye.

1690—M. de Louvigny.

1694—M. Antione de la Motte-Cadillac.

1715—M. de Vaudreuil (In doubt).

1718 or 1728—M. de Louvigny.   (In dispute as to whether at St. Ignace or Mackinaw City).

MACKINAW CITY

1742—Mons. de Blainville.

1744—Mons. de Vivehevet.

Mons. de Ramelia.

1745—Duplessis de Morampont.

Noyelle, Jr.

Capt. Louis de la Corne.

1747—Mons. de Noyelle, Jr.

1748—Capt. Jacques Legardeur de St. Pierre.

1749—Chevalier de Repentigy.

Mons. Godfroy.

1750—Capt. Duplessis Faber.

1751—Mons. Duplessis, Jr.

1753—Capt. Beaujeu de Villemonde.

1754—Capt. Herben.

1755—Chevalier Louis Legardeur.

1756—Charles de L'Anglade.

1760—M. de Beaujian.

Indians and LaSalle's "Griffin."

THE SECOND
FORT MICHILIMACKINAC
At Mackinaw City

CHAPTER ONE

As stated in the preceding chapter, the date of the location and building of Fort Michilimackinac at Mackinaw City remains a mystery yet unsolved. Henry R. Schoolcraft, the great student, historian and Indian agent, said in 1820: "We visited the ancient site of Fort Michilimackinac, a spot celebrated in the early missionary annals and history of New France. The mission of St. Ignace had been attempted on the north shore of the Straits, but was finally removed here".

Some authorities claim that when Father Marest returned from Montreal in 1708, a few years after the evacuation of St. Ignace by Cadillac, he began a new mission at Mackinaw City, and that it was there that M. Louvigny came with his garrison about 1712, or, as one chronicler insists, in 1728.

We do know that some years previous to 1740 the French established a fort, garrison, trading post and mission at Mackinaw City. The location is at the apex of the lower Michigan peninsula at the point where the Straits of Mackinac flow into Lake Michigan on the west, and is flanked on the east by the great bay (the "south passage of the Straits of Mackinac") which extends south to the harbor of Cheboygan. Writing his interesting but somewhat conflicting history in 1860, W. P. Strickland said: "The commanding position of Mackinaw City, although always known to the

Indians, missionaries and traders, and lately confirmed by European military tacticians, is as yet not perceived by the government of the United States." At Mackinaw City the land rises gradually from the lake level until it reaches an elevation of seventy five feet, "from which point beautiful and picturesque views are obtained of the Strait, with the numerous islands sleeping on its bosom."

Certain it is that Mackinaw City had been the theater of some of the most interesting events in Indian history before the coming of the "white man". It was the metropolis of a part of the Ojibway, Huron and Ottawa nations, where councils of war and peace were held. Its mainland location made it available for trails into the Indian country further south, and, because of the narrow limits of the width of the Straits of Mackinac, it was a strategic and important point for both the peaceful pursuits of trade and the strategies of war.

Few will dispute the fact that Fort Michilimackinac was built over two hundred years ago on the same location, and with the same outlines, which the reconstructed fort has today. The French designed it after the lessons they had learned at St. Ignace, in the British re-construction and re-occupation later on was identically the same, and the restoration of 1933 disclosed the exactness of the re-survey, as will be shown later in this narrative.

The old fort enclosed two or three acres, and was constructed of long and heavy stakes or pickets on the general primitive stockade plan. The accompanying pictures emphasize the story of its construction. It was built of "pickets of cedar wood, and so near the water's edge that, when the wind is in the west, waves break against the stockade."

Within or near the enclosures of the original fort the aggressive Jesuits erected a mission chapel and a "college", the first institution of learning, if it may so be called, along the northwest frontier. Here also were the great depots used by the coureurs de bois for stocking the goods they brought from Canada for the fur trade with the Indians. Outside the stockade the Red men had their villages, and on an eminence not far from the fort the Ottawas erected a crude fortification of their own.

It must be remembered that there was almost constant warring among the northwest Indian tribes, although in emergencies they banded together against the fierce Iroquois, their common enemy. The latter were the allies, in most years, of the British, who occupied and commanded New York and the Hudson river country. English eyes turned covetously to the great French and Indian fur trade of the north, and the boldest of English traders strayed far from their own bailiwick in reaching for a share of this profitable business.

So it was that the British lost no time in turning their attention to the northwest territory immediately after the defeat of the French under Montcalm in the famous battle of Quebec in 1759, where General Wolfe died at the moment of his greatest victory. The battle of Quebec tolled the last bell for French control of Canada and the northwest. The British came at once into possession and within

less than a year a garrison marched through the
gates of Fort Michilimackinac at Mackinaw City.
The French archives show that "Monsieur de Beaujeau, formerly captain in command at Michilimackinac, evacuated that post in the month of October,
1760, after the taking of Montreal, in order to retire to the Illinois, with four officers, two cadets,
forty eight soldiers and seventy eight militia."

CHAPTER TWO

Soldiers of England had promptly taken possession of the fort at Detroit, this expedition being under command of Major Robert Rogers, later to make history at Fort Michilimackinac. The then Indian ally of the British was the great Indian chief Pontiac, soon to become their most bitter enemy.

After garrisoning Detroit, Major Rogers started with his soldiers to take over at Mackinaw City, but it was late in the season and severe weather drove the command back to Detroit. So for over a year after the departure of de Beaujeau and his troops Old Mackinaw was occupied without contest by French traders, who vigorously continued their fur trade with the Indians, taking care to strengthen their friendship with the various tribes against the days of English competition and control. The French soldiers had gone; no English garrison had come.

At this time some of the leaders of the French traders and their Indians at Fort Michilimackinac seriously considered a re-possession of their own, involving the strengthening of the local fortifications and raising once more the flag of France. This scheme was quickly snuffed out when an Indian runner reported that English soldiers from Fort Detroit were on the way north, and actually only five miles south of Mackinaw.

The very next morning the British garrison, as predicted, arrived to take over Fort Michilimackinac. The soldiers were under the command of Major George Etherington, who had served with some distinction under Wolfe on the plains of Abraham and in the capture of Quebec. It is uncertain how large a military company made up this garrison. Probably some two hundred or more at first, to be reduced by details sent to Green Bay and other forts later. The officers and their men occupied the thirty cabins inside the fort or stockade.

We introduce the reader now to one of the famous characters of early Straits history—the English trader and soldier of fortune, Alexander Henry. This educated and courageous pioneer has given us the best account of one of the most thrilling periods in all the stirring history of the northwest. Henry was trading at Mackinac Island when the end came to French control. He says: "I found the Island inhabited by a large village of Indians, and we remained friendly until, discovering that I was an Englishman, they told my men that the Indians at Michilimackinac would not fail to kill me, and that, therefore, they had a right to share in the pillage. The hostility of the Indians was exclusively against the English. Between the Indians and my French Canadian attendants there appeared to be the most cordial good will."

Henry decided to "change his nationality" and assumed a costume characteristic of the French courier de bois, smearing his face "with dirt and grease" and donning a "large red, milled worsted cap." He had the courage to go on to the mainland at Old Mackinaw, but turned over his goods and chattels to his trusted assistant, Campion, for the Indian barter and trade, seeking for himself some degree of privacy in a friendly Frenchman's cabin, after instructing his men to conceal the fact that he was English.

Here we may well turn to the history written by Alexander Henry himself and elaborations there-on taken from the "Historic Mackinac" of that eminent author and civic leader, the late Edwin O. Wood, 1913-1916 president of the Mackinac Island State Park Commission, published in 1918 by the Macmillan Company of New York, and now out of print. We take up this thread of the story after Alexander Henry's chilly reception from the Indians on Mackinac Island, his speedy departure and the arrival of his canoes at Mackinaw on the mainland, freely quoting from the Wood history:

On arriving at Mackinaw Campion had found a house, to which Henry retired, "but the men soon betrayed my secret, and I was visited by the inhabitants, with great show of curiosity. They assured me that I could not stay at Michilimackinac without the most imminent risk, and strongly recommended that I should lose no time in making my escape to Detroit."

Though this advice made him uneasy, "it did not shake my determination to remain with my property and encounter the evils with which I was threatened; and my spirits were in some measure sustained by the sentiments of Campion in this regard, for he declared his belief that the Canadian inhabitants of the fort were more hostile than the

Indians, as being jealous of English traders, who, like myself, were penetrating into the country."

Scarcely was he relieved from the admonitions of the inhabitants of the fort, when he was informed that the whole band of Chippewas from Mackinac Island had arrived with the intention of paying him a visit.

"There was, in the fort, one Farley, an interpreter, lately in the employ of the French Commandant. He had married a Chippeway woman, and was said to possess great influence over the nation to which his wife belonged. Doubtful as to the kind of visit which I was about to receive, I sent for this interpreter, and requested, first, that he would have the kindness to be present at the interview, and, secondly, that he would inform me of the intentions of the band. M. Farley agreed to be present, and as to the object of the visit, replied, that it was consistent with uniform custom, that a stranger on his arrival should be waited upon, and welcomed, by the chiefs of the nation, who, on their part, always gave a small present, and always expected a large one; but, as to the rest, declared himself unable to answer for the particular views of the Chippeways, on this occasion, I being an Englishman, and the Indians having made no treaty with the English. He thought that there might be danger, the Indians having protested that they would not suffer an Englishman to remain in their part of the country."

This information was far from agreeable, but Henry determined to await the outcome with fortitude and patience.

"At two o'clock in the afternoon, the Chippeways came to my house, about sixty in number, and headed by Mina'va'va'na', their chief. They walked in single file, each with his tomahawk in one hand, and scalping knife in the other. Their bodies were naked, from the waist upward; except in a few exceptions, where blankets were thrown loosely over the shoulders. Their faces were painted with charcoal, worked up with grease; their bodies, with white clay, in patterns of various fancies. Some had feathers thrust through their noses, and their heads decorated with the same. It is unnecessary to dwell on the sensations with which I beheld the approach of this uncouth, if not frightful assemblage.

CHAPTER THREE

"The chief entered first; and the rest followed, without noise. On receiving a sign from the former, the latter seated themselves on the floor.

Minavavana appeared about fifty years of age. He was six feet in height, and had, in his countenance, an indescribable mixture of good and evil. Looking steadfastly at me, where I sat in ceremony with an interpreter on either hand, and several Canadians behind me, he entered at the same time into conversation with Campion, inquiring how long it was since I left Montreal, and observing that the English, as it would seem, were brave men, and not afraid of death, since they had dared to come, as I had done, fearlessly among their enemies.

"The Indians now gravely smoked their pipes, while I inwardly endured the tortures of suspense. At length, the pipes being finished, as well as a long pause, by which they were succeeded, Minavavana, taking a few strings of wampum in his hand, began the following speech:

"Englishman, it to you that I speak, and I demand your attention!

"Englishman, you know that the French King is our father. He promised to be such; and we, in return, promised to be his children. This promise we have kept.

"Englishman, it is you who have made war with this, our father. You are his enemy; and how then could you have the boldness to venture among us, his children? You know that his enemies are ours.

"Englishman, we are informed that our father, the King of France, is old and infirm; and that, being fatigued with making war upon your nation he has fallen asleep. During his sleep you have taken advantage of him and possessed yourselves of Canada. But his nap is almost at an end. I think I hear him already stirring and enquiring for his children, the Indians. When he does awake, what must become of you?

"Englishman, although you have conquered the French you have not conquered us. We are not your slaves. These woods, these lakes, these hills were left to us by our ancestors. They are our inheritance; and we will part with them to no one. Your nation supposes that we, like the white people, cannot live without bread and pork and beef. But the Great Spirit has provided food for us in these spacious lakes and wooded hills.

"Englishman, our father, the King of France, employed our young men to make war upon your nation. In that war many of them have been killed, and it is our custom to retaliate until the spirits of the slain are sat'sfied. But the spirits of the slain are only to be satisfied in one of two ways; the first is by spilling of the blood of the nation by which they fell; the other by covering the bodies of the dead, and thus allaying the resentment of their relatives. This is done by making presents.

"Englishman: Your king has never sent us any presents, nor entered into any treaty with us, wherefore he and we are still at war. Until he does these things we must consider that we have no other father nor friend among the white man than the King of France. But for you we have taken into consideration that you have ventured your life among us, coming to us unarmed in the expectation that we would not molest you. You do not come armed with an intention to make war; you come in peace to trade with us and supply the necessities which we so much want. We shall regard you, therefore, as a brother, and you may sleep peacefully without fear of the Chippeways. As a token of our friendship we present you this pipe to smoke."

By the aid of his interpreter, Henry replied to Minavavana's speech, that only the good character he heard of the Indians had emboldened him to come among them; that their father, the King of England, would be as good to them as the King of France had been. The Indians seemed satisfied, and Henry distributed presents among them. He assorted his goods, and prepared to accompany his agents to trade in the surrounding country.

But new dangers arose, coming from a village of the Ottawas at L'Arbre Croche, about twenty miles west of Old Mackinaw. Just as he was about to set out, two hundred Ottawa warriors entered the fort, and the next day ordered him to appear before their council. He complied, and one of the chiefs addressed the assembly, expressing pleasure at having heard of Henry's arrival with goods the Indians needed, but surprise that these goods were now about to be sent elsewhere, even to their enemies. He demanded on behalf of his people, that Henry

deliver to them merchandise and ammunition to
the amount of fifty beaver-skins, on credit, to be
paid for the following summer. Henry had learned
that the Ottawas never paid for what they received
on credit. The only concession the Indians would
make was one day for reflection, at the end of
which they would, if need be, seize the goods,
which they considered already forfeited, since the
goods had been brought into their country before
the conclusion of any peace with the English.

The interpreter informed Henry that the Ottawas intended to kill him that night unless he complied with their demands: but Henry and his party
armed themselves in their house and the night
passed without an attack. When the traders were
summoned to a council the next morning, they refused to attend. Towards sunset that night, they
learned from Campion, the Frenchman, that a detachment of English troops, sent to garrison the
fort, was only five miles away and would arrive
next morning. After a watchful and anxious night,
the Ottawas were seen at daybreak taking their departure."

An eminent colonial authority, Franklin B.
Hough, thus describes the general state of mind
along the frontier between the years 1760, when
Fort Michilimackinac came under British control,
and the tragic events of 1763 at this historic post:
"It will be remembered that the French still retained control and command of the posts upon the
Mississippi; that most of the inhabitants of this section who were scattered around the military posts
of the interior, garrisoned by English troops, were

Schneider's working model for reconstruction of Old Fort Michilimackinac at Mackinaw City.

still living in terms of intimacy with the Indians and, although yielding a formal allegiance to their new (British) masters, were still antagonistic in heart and language. French missionaries and emissaries were also residing in the Indian villages. The war between France and England was still raging in Europe, although ended in America, and a series of successes in the Old World might have still permitted the French to claim the relinquishment back to them of their former holdings in Canada.

"The Indians had been taught by their French allies that the King of France was scarcely less omnipotent than Diety, and that he loved and would protect his Red children. Here is sufficient reason and background for the war which devastated the northwest frontiers in the summer of 1763, and in which Pontiac, the great Ottawa chief, was the leading spirit."

From the beginning of the English colonization of America, representatives of the British king had, with few exceptions, entirely disregarded the rights and feelings of the Indians. The French had been, as a rule, kindly and considerate. The sequel was at hand.

CHAPTER FOUR

The great Ottawa warrior and chieftain, Pontiac, then about fifty years of age, had become the principal leader of nearly all the Indian tribes of the Algonquin stock. He was their spokesman in peace as well as war. In battle he had shown his courage; in council his eloquence and wisdom. He was wary in planning and indefatigable in execution, nursing meantime a great ambition for power and place. Although a life time friend and ally of the French, he hastened to confer with Major Rogers when the tri-colors had been lowered in defeat. Pontiac sensed that the French were through in the northwest, and believed that the English would give him rank, power and prestige in keeping with his ambitions. He is reported to have demanded the pay, rank and uniform of a British general, all of which were most bluntly refused.

Pondering his personal slight and brooding over the wrongs of his own people, Pontiac planned a master stroke, which he believed would forever drive out the British from the American frontier. Acquired from the French or established within the British original territory were forts or posts around the Great Lakes, and their vicinity, located at Detroit, Michilimackinac, Fort Pitt, Green Bay, Ouiatenon, St. Joseph, Maumee, Sandusky, Niagara, Presque Isle, Venango and Le Bueof. Five of these were strongly protected forts, the remainder trading posts with little fortified protection.

Pontiac conceived a concerted surprise attack upon all these points by his Indians on June 4th, 1763, the birthday of King George the Third of England. Emissaries were sent to Indian villages far and near, bitterly eloquent tirades were made around a hundred camp fires against the "Red Coats", and the war dances were quickly on. Many places Pontiac personally visited and by his stirring eloquence aroused the braves to a frenzy of revenge and massacre. Squaws were set at the task of making bullets, mixing war paint and sharpening knives and tomahawks. The great climax of preparation came at a council of all the Indian chiefs, called by Pontiac near Detroit on April 27th, 1763.

After the council preliminaries were over Pontiac, in full regalia of warfare, addressed his fierce auditors with an impassioned appeal. Each time he paused, deep and gutteral ejaculations of approval came from his painted hearers. He inveighed against the arrogance, cupidity and injustice of the English, comparing them in contrast with the French, whom they had driven from the territory. Then, holding up a broad belt of wampum, Pontiac told the council that he had received it from the King of France, their great and kindly father; that the sleep of the French was at an end; and that the great war canoes of the King would soon sail up the St. Lawrence, to win back Canada and wreak vengeance upon all enemies.

Norman B. Wood, authority on Indian lore, tells us the aftermath of this conspiracy, "constructed with the white man's skill and the red man's

cunning". The plan was now ripe for execution,
and with the suddenness and fury of a whirlwind
the storm of war broke all along the frontier. "Nine
of the British forts were captured. Some of the
garrisons were completely massacred, while in other
cases a scattering few escaped." Of all the tragic
scenes enacted, the most bloody and savage was
within the limits of Fort Michilimackinac at Mackinaw City.

For three years Major Etherington had commanded the fort at Old Mackinaw. His garrison
had been reduced by transfers and illness to some
ninety-five officers and men, including his two jun-
iors, Lieutenants Jemette and Lesslie. The life at
the fort for those three years had been comparative-
ly quiet and uneventful. The Indians remained
surly, but never-the-less maintained their trading in
furs, and there was always some sort of Indian en-
campment outside the stockade. A considerable
number of French traders made the post their permanent home, living in cabins outside the fort.

Late in May, 1763, and at the turn of the
month to June, groups of Indians drifted into old
Mackinaw and made camp. Their number increased to several hundred with unexplained suddenness. A famous trader, Charles de Langlade, being
at old Mackinaw after gathering here and there
rumors of an intended attack, hastened to warn
Major Etherington of the plot against the English.
The commandant sent for some of the chiefs and
swallowed without hesitation their denials, and accepted their protestations of friendship. A day
later Langlade, with Alexander Henry, Laurent

Ducharme, a Canadian, and others again warned the British officer, so arousing his ire that he threatened to imprison in the guard house the next man who mentioned an Indian uprising. He felt secure with his garrison of nearly one hundred, all of whom were well armed.

Pontiac had assigned the task of surprising and capturing Fort Michilimackinac to his allies, the fierce Ojibways under Chief Minavavana, a bitter hater of the English. When the French went down in defeat four years previously Minavavana had sworn that he would ever remain an unreconciled enemy to the British. This stern and cruel warrior arrived at Old Mackinaw at the time appointed. With other chiefs he suggested to Major Etherington that the Indians would like to celebrate the King's birthday on June 4th with a friendly game of Baug-ah-ud-o-way (we know it as la crosse), the young men of the Ojibways contesting with the Osaugee tribe in an exhibition of skill, for a very substantial prize.

The British commandant fell quickly into the trap, and the next day, June 4, 1763, the game was begun in the open spaces east of the main entrance to the fort. The gates of the stockade were swung wide open, and about them gathered the blanketed squaws to watch the contest. Outside the entrance the officers occupied places of vantage, and within the fort the soldiers viewed the game from the platforms lining the stockade. The game had been on for only a short time when, by preconcerted plan, the ball was thrown inside the fort, with the Indians of both teams in hot pursuit. As they passed through the gates, guns, knives and hatchets were snatched from beneath the squaws' blankets and the massacre started.

In a few bloody moments a lieutenant and sixty-five soldiers had been butchered and scalped, while outside the fort the commandant and some twenty of his men had been made captives, stripped of their clothing and bound to convenient trees. The fierce Ojibways, supposed to have been the only American Indians addicted to cannibalism, let the captives know that they were being kept for a great feast and victory celebration. Later, however, through the interference of the less warlike Ottawas, Major Etherington went free, with a few soldiers who had survived. Alexander Henry also escaped death and appears again in safety on Mackinac Island after he had been "purchased" by extensive gifts presented to his captors by Chief Wawassom, Henry's friend and "blood brother."

There is much discrepancy between the accounts of this massacre written by Henry, the English trader, and Etherington, the English commandant. However, since the major's two military reports differed in material points regarding the losses of life and other circumstances of this bloody affair, most historians have inclined to the story related by Henry.

Be that as it may, there was a bloody massacre, the British were driven out or killed, but the Indians did not destroy or burn the fort itself, nor did they molest the French traders and their families, totalling several hundred souls. As a matter of fact, it was through the kindly intervention of a French

priest that Major Etherington was spared. The
Pontiac rebellion missed its main objective, but, so
far as the Michilimackinac region was concerned, it
drove out for the time being every British soldier
and depopulated or destroyed every English fort.

CHAPTER FIVE

The foregoing account of the Pontiac massacre at Fort Michilimackinac at what is now Mackinaw City is based on the best available facts obtainable from the somewhat fragmentary history, full of conflicting reports, which has come to us from the few authorities of nearly two centuries ago.

However, the story of this foul conspiracy and bloody massacre is so characteristic of the early days in the Northwest frontier, and so many thousand seasonal visitors today go to Mackinaw City State Park to examine for themselves the accurately reconstructed old fort, just as it appeared on the morning of June 4, 1763, one hundred and seventy-five years ago, that we venture to reproduce here the story as written by Alexander Henry himself, in the later period of his retirement, and published in book form many years ago. Copies are rare in even the great metropolitan libraries. Perhaps the Henry story is somewhat embellished, but if the reader desires at first hand an autobiographical "western", enacted and written a century or more ago, he will be glad to peruse the doughty old Englishman's narrative in his own words, which here follow:

"Shortly after my first arrival at Michilimackinac, in the preceding year," says Henry, "a Chipeway, named Wa'wa'tam, began to come often to my house, betraying in his demeanor strong marks of personal regard. After this had continued for some time, he came, on a certain day, bringing with him his whole family, at the same time a large present, consisting of skins, sugar and dried meat. Having laid these in a heap, he commenced a speech, in which he informed me, that some years before, he had observed a fast, devoting himself, according to the custom of his nation, to solitude, and to the mortification of his body, in the hope to obtain, from the Great Spirit, protection through all his days; that on this occasion, he had dreamed of adopting an Englishman, as his son, brother and friend; that from the moment in which he first beheld me, he had recognized me as the person whom the Great Spirit had been pleased to point out to him for a brother; that he hoped that I would not refuse his present; and that he should forever regard me as one of his family.

"I could not do otherwise than accept the present, and declare my willingness to have so good a man, as this appeared to be, for my friend and brother. I offered a present in return for that which I had received, which Wawatam accepted, and then, thanking me for the favor which he said that I had rendered him, he left me, and soon after set out on his winter's hunt.

"Twelve months had now elapsed, since the occurrence of this incident, and I had almost forgotten the person of my brother, when, on the second day of June, 1763, Wawatam came again to my house, in a temper of mind visibly melancholy and thoughtful. He told me that he had just returned from his wintering-ground, and I asked after his health; but, without answering my question, he went on to say, that he was very sorry to find me returned from the Sault; that he had intended to go to that place himself, immediately after his arrival at Michilimackinac; and that he wished me to go there, along with him and his family, the next morning. To all this, he joined an inquiry, whether or not the commandant had heard bad news, adding, that, during the winter, he had himself been frequently disturbed with the noise of evil birds; and further suggesting, that there were numerous Indians near the fort, many of whom had never shown themselves within it. Wawatam was about forty-five years of age, of an excellent character among his nation, and a chief.

"Referring much of what I had heard to the peculiarities of the Indian character, I did not pay all the attention which they will be found to have deserved, to the entreaties and remarks of my visitor. I answered that I could not think of going to the Sault, so soon as the next morning, but would follow him there, after the arrival of my clerks. Finding himself unable to prevail with me, he withdrew, for that day; but, early the next morning, he came again, bringing with him his wife, and a present of dried meat. At this interview, after stating that he had several packs of beaver, for which he intended to deal with me, he expressed, a second time, his apprehensions, from the numerous Indians who were round the fort, and earnestly pressed me to consent to an immediate departure for the Sault. As a reason for this particular request, he assured me that all the Indians proposed to come in a body, that day, to the fort, to demand liquor of the commandant, and that he wished me to be gone, before they should grow intoxicated.

"I had made, at the period to which I am now referring, so much progress in the language in which Wawatam addressed me, as to be able to hold an ordinary conversation in it; but, the Indian manner of speech is so extravagantly figurative, that it is only for a very perfect master to follow and comprehend it entirely. Had I been further advanced in this respect, I think that I should have gathered so much information, from this my friendly monitor, as would have put me into possession of the design of the enemy, and enabled me to save as well others as myself; as it was, it unfortunately happened, that I turned a deaf ear to everything, leaving Wawatam and his wife, after long and patient, but ineffectual efforts, to depart alone, with dejected countenances, and not before they had each let fall some tears.

"In the course of the same day, I observed that the Indians came in great numbers into the fort, purchasing tomahawks (small axes, of one pound weight) and frequently desiring to see silver armbands, and other valuable ornaments, of which I had a large quantity for sale. These ornaments, however, they in no instance purchased; but, after turning them over, left them, saying that they would call again the next day. Their motive, as it afterward appeared, was no other than the very artful one of discovering, by requesting to see them, the particular places of their deposit, so that they might lay their hands on them in the moment of pillage with the greater certainty and dispatch.

"At night, I turned in my mind the visits of Wawatam; but, although they were calculated to excite uneasiness, nothing induced me to believe that serious mischief was at hand. The next day, being the fourth of June, was the king's birthday.

"The morning was sultry. A Chipeway came to tell me that his nation was going to play at bag'gat'-iway, with the Sacs or Saakies, another Indian nation, for a high wager. He invited me to witness the sport, adding that the commandant was to be there, and would bet on the side of the Chipeways. In consequence of this information, I went to the commandant, and expostulated with him a little, representing that the Indians might possibly have some sinister end in view; but, the commandant only smiled at my suspicions.

"Baggatiway, called by the Canadians, le jeu de la crosse, is played with a bat and ball. The bat is about four feet in length, curved, and terminating in a sort of racket. Two posts are planted in the ground, at a considerable distance from each other, as a mile, or more. Each party has its post, and the game consists in throwing the ball up to the post of the adversary. The ball, at the beginning, is placed in the middle of the course, and each party endeavors as well to throw the ball out of the direction of its own post, as into that of the adversary's.

"I did not go myself to see the match which was now to be played without the fort, because, there being a canoe prepared to depart, on the following day, for Montreal, I employed myself in writing letters to my friends; and even when a fel-

Airplane view of restored Fort Michilimackinac at Mackinaw City.

low-trader, Mr. Tracy, happened to call upon me, saying that another canoe had just arrived from Detroit, and proposing that I should go with him to the beach, to inquire the news, it so happened that I still remained, to finish my letters; promising to follow Mr. Tracy in the course of a few minutes. Mr. Tracy had not gone more than twenty paces from my door, when I heard an Indian war-cry, and a noise of general confusion.

"Going instantly to my window, I saw a crowd of Indians, within the fort, furiously cutting down and scalping every Englishman they found. In particular, I witnessed the fate of Lieutenant Jemette.

"I had, in the room in which I was, a fowling-piece, loaded with swan-shot. This I immediately seized, and held it for a few minutes, waiting to hear the drum beat to arms. In this dreadful interval I saw several of my countrymen fall, and more than one struggling between the knees of an Indian, who, holding him in this manner, scalped him, while yet living.

"At length, disappointed in the hope of seeing resistance made to the enemy, and sensible, of course, that no effort of my own unassisted arm, could avail against four hundred Indians, I thought only of seeking shelter. Amid the slaughter which was raging, I observed many of the Canadian inhabitants of the fort, calmly looking on, neither opposing the Indians, nor suffering injury; and, from this circumstance, I conceived a hope of finding security in their houses.

"Between the yard-door of my own house, and that of M. Langlade, my next neighbour, there was only a low fence, over which I easily climbed. At my entrance, I found the whole family at the windows, gazing at the scene of blood before them. I addressed myself immediately to M. Langlade, begging that he would put me into some place of safety, until the heat of the affair should be over; an act of charity by which he might perhaps preserve me from the general massacre; but while I uttered my petition, M. Langlade, who had looked for a moment at me, turned again to the window, shrugging his shoulders, and intimating that he could do nothing for me: 'Que voudriezvous que j'en ferais?'

"This was a moment of despair; but the next, a Pani woman, a slave of M. Langlade's, beckoned to me to follow her. She brought me to a door, which she opened, desiring me to enter, and telling me that it led to the garret, where I must go and conceal myself. I joyfully obeyed her directions; and she, having followed me up to the garret door, locked it after me, and with great presence of mind took away the key.

"This shelter obtained, if shelter I could hope to find it, I was naturally anxious to know what might still be passing without. Through an aperture, which afforded me a view of the area of the fort, I beheld, in shapes the foulest and most terrible, the ferocious triumphs of barbarian conquerors. The dead were scalped and mangled; the dying were writhing and shrieking, under the unsatiated knife and tomahawk; and, from the bodies of some ripped open, their butchers were drinking the blood, scooped up in the hollow of joined hands, and quaffed amid shouts of rage and victory. I was shaken, not only with horror, but with fear. The sufferings which I had witnessed, I seemed on the point of experiencing. No long time elapsed, before every one being destroyed, who could be found, there was a general cry of 'All is finished!' At the same instant, I heard some of the Indians enter the house in which I was.

CHAPTER SIX

"The garret was separated from the room below, only by a layer of single boards, at once the flooring of the one and the ceiling of the other. I could therefore hear everything that passed; and, the Indians no sooner in, than they inquired whether or not any Englishmen were in the house? M. Langlade replied that 'He could not say—he did not know of any;'—answers in which he did not exceed the truth; for the Pani woman had not only hidden me by stealth, but kept my secret, and her own. M. Langlade was therefore, as I presume, as far from a wish to destroy me, as he was careless about saving me, when he added to these answers, that 'They might examine for themselves, and would soon be satisfied, as to the object of their question.' Saying this, he brought them to the garret door.

"The state of my mind will be imagined. Arrived at the door, some delay was occasioned by the absence of the key, and a few moments were thus allowed me, in which to look around for a hiding place. In one corner of the garret was a heap of those vessels of birch-bark, used in maple-sugar making, as I have recently described.

"The door was unlocked, and opening, and the Indians ascending the stairs before I had completely crept into a small opening, which presented itself, at one end of the heap. An instant after, four Indians entered the room, all armed with tomahawks, and all besmeared with blood, upon every part of their bodies.

"The die appeared to be cast. I could scarcely breathe; but I thought that the throbbing of my heart occasioned a noise loud enough to betray me. The Indians walked in every direction about the garret, and one of them approached me so closely that at a particular moment, had he put out his hand he must have touched me. Still, I remained undiscovered; a circumstance to which the dark color of my clothes, and the corner in which I was, must have contributed. In a word, after taking several turns in the room, during want of light, in a room which had no window, and in which they told M. Langlade how many they had killed and how many scalps they had taken, they returned down stairs, and I, with sensations not to be expressed, heard the door, which was the barrier between me and my fate, locked for the second time.

"There was a feather-bed on the floor; and, on this, exhausted as I was, by the agitation of my mind, I threw myself down and fell asleep. In this state I remained till the dusk of the evening, when I was awakened by a second opening of the door. The person that now entered was M. Langlade's wife, who was much surprised at finding me, but advised me not to be uneasy, observing that the Indians had killed most of the English, but that she hoped I might myself escape. A shower of rain having begun to fall, she had come to stop a hole in the roof. On her going away, I begged her to send me a little water, which she did.

"As night was now advancing, I continued to lie on the bed, ruminating on my condition, but unable to discover a resource, from which I could hope for life. A flight, to Detroit, had no probable chance of success. The distance, from Michilimackinac, was four hundred miles; I was without provisions; and the whole length of the road lay through Indian countries, countries of an enemy in arms, where the first man whom I should meet would kill me. To stay where I was, threatened nearly the same issue. As before, fatigue of mind, and not tranquillity, suspended my cares, and procured me further sleep. . . .

"The respite which sleep afforded me, during the night, was put an end to by the return of morning. I was again on the rack of apprehension. At sunrise, I heard the family stirring; and, presently after, Indian voices, informing M. Langlade that they had not found my hapless self among the dead, and that they supposed me to be somewhere concealed. M. Langlade appeared, from what followed, to be, by this time, acquainted with the place of my retreat, of which, no doubt, he had been informed by his wife. The poor woman, as soon as the Indians mentioned me declared to her husband in the French tongue, that he should no longer keep me in his house, but deliver me up to my pursuers; giving as a reason for this measure, that should the Indians discover his instrumentality in my concealment, they might revenge it on her children, and that it was better that I should die than they. M. Langlade resisted, at first, this sentence of his wife's; but soon suffered her to prevail, informing the Indians that he had been told I was in his house, that I had come there without his knowledge, and that he would put me into their hands. This was no sooner expressed that he began to ascend the stairs, the Indians following upon his heels.

"I now resigned myself to the fate with which I was menaced; and, regarding every attempt at concealment as vain, I arose from the bed and presented myself full in view, to the Indians who were entering the room. They were all in a state of intoxication, and entirely naked, except about the middle. One of them, named Wenniway, whom I had previously known, and who was upward of six feet in height, had his entire body covered with charcoal and grease, only that a white spot, of two inches in diameter, encircled either eye. This man, walking up to me, seized me, with one hand, by the collar of the coat, while in the other hand he held a large carving knife, as if to plunge it in my breast; his eyes, meanwhile, were fixed steadfastly on mine. At length, after some seconds, of the most anxious suspense, he dropped his arm, saying, 'I won't kill you!' To this he added that he had been frequently engaged in wars against the English, and had brought away many scalps; that, on a certain occasion, he had lost a brother, whose name was Musinigon, and that I should be called after him.

"A reprieve, upon any terms, placed me among the living, and gave me back the sustaining voice of hope; but Wenniway ordered me down stairs, and there informing me that I was to be taken to his cabin, where, and indeed every where else, the Indians were all mad with liquor, death again

was threatened, and not as possible only, but as
certain. I mentioned my fears upon this subject to
M. Langlade, begging him to represent the danger
to my master. M. Langlade, in this instance, did
not with-hold his compassion, and Wenniway immediately consented that I should remain where I
was, until he found another opportunity to take me
away.

"Thus far secure, I re-ascended my garret-
stairs, in order to place myself, the furthest possible,
out of the reach of insult from drunken Indians;
but I had not remained there more than an hour,
when I was called to the room below, in which was
an Indian, who said that I must go with him out of
the fort, Wenniway having sent him to fetch me.
This man, as well as Wenniway himself, I had seen
before. In the preceding year, I had allowed him
to take goods on credit, for which he was still in my
debt; and some short time previous to the surprise
of the fort he had said, upon my upbraiding him
with want of honesty, that 'He would pay me "before long!" ' This speech now came afresh into my
memory, and led me to suspect that the fellow had
formed a design against my life. I communicated
the suspicion to M. Langlade; but he gave for
answer, that 'I was not now my own master,' and
must 'do as I was ordered.'

"The Indian, on his part, directed that before I
left the house, I should undress myself, declaring
that my coat and shirt would become him better
than they did me. His pleasure, in this respect,
being complied with, no other alternative was left
me than either to go out naked, or to put on the

clothes of the Indian, which he freely gave me in exchange. His motive, for thus stripping me of my own apparel, was no other, as I afterward learned, than this, that it might not be stained with blood when he should kill me.

"I was now told to proceed; and my driver followed me close, until I had passed the gate of the fort, when I turned toward the spot where I knew the Indians to be encamped. This, however, did not suit the purpose of my enemy, who seized me by the arm, and drew me violently, in the opposite direction, to the distance of fifty yards, above the fort. Here, finding that I was approaching the bushes and sandhills, I determined to proceed no further, but told the Indian that I believed he meant to murder me, and that if so, he might as well strike where I was, as at any greater distance. He replied, with coolness, that my suspicions were just, and that he meant to pay me, in this manner, for my goods. At the same time, he produced a knife, and held me in a position to receive the intended blow. Both this, and that which followed, were necessarily the affair of a moment. By some effort, too sudden and too little dependent on thought, to be explained or remembered, I was enabled to arrest his arm, and give him a sudden push, by which I turned him from me, and released myself from his grasp. This was no sooner done, than I ran toward the fort, with all the swiftness in my power, the Indian following me, and I expecting every moment to feel his knife. I succeeded in my flight, and on entering the fort, I saw Wenniway, standing in the midst of the area, and to him I hastened for protection. Wenniway desired the Indian to desist; but the latter pursued me round him, making several strokes at me with his knife, and foaming at the mouth, with rage at the repeated failure of his purpose. At length, Wenniway drew near to M. Langlade's house; and, the door being open, I ran into it. The Indian followed me; but, on my entering the house, he voluntarily abandoned the pursuit.

"Preserved so often, and so unexpectedly, as it now had been my lot to be, I returned to my garret with a strong inclination to believe, that through the will of an overruling power, no Indian enemy could do me hurt; but, new trials, as I believed, were at hand, when, at ten o'clock in the evening, I was roused from sleep, and once more desired to descend the stairs. Not less, however, to my satisfaction than surprise, I was summoned only to meet Major Etherington, Mr. Bostwick and Lieutenant Leslie, who were in the room below.

"These gentlemen had been taken prisoners, while looking at the game, without the fort, and immediately stripped of all their clothes. They were now sent into the fort, under the charge of Canadians, because, the Indians having resolved on getting drunk, the chiefs were apprehensive that they would be murdered, if they continued in the camp. Lieutenant Jemette and seventy soldiers had been killed; and but twenty Englishmen, including soldiers, were still alive. These were all within the fort, together with nearly three hundred Canadians.

"These being our numbers, myself and others proposed to Major Etherington, to make an effort for regaining possession of the fort, and maintaining it against the Indians. The Jesuit missionary was consulted on the subject; but he discouraged us, by his representations, not only of the merciless treatment which we must expect from the Indians, should they regain their superiority, but of the little dependence which was to be placed upon our Canadian auxiliaries. Thus, the fort and prisoners remained in the hands of the Indians, though, through the whole night, the prisoners and whites were in actual possession, and they were without the gates.

"That whole night, or the greater part of it, was passed in mutual condolence; and my fellow prisoners shared my garret. In the morning, being again called down, I found my master, Wenniway, and was desired to follow him. He led me to a small house, within the fort, where, in a narrow room, and almost dark, I found Mr. Ezekiel Solomons, an Englishman from Detroit, and a soldier, all prisoners. With these, I remained in painful suspense, as to the scene that was next to present itself, till ten o'clock, in the forenoon, when an Indian arrived, and presently marched us to the lake-side, where a canoe appeared ready for departure, and in which we found we were to embark.

"Our voyage, full of doubt as it was, would have commenced immediately, but that one of the Indians, who was to be of the party, was absent. His arrival was to be waited for; and this occasioned a very long delay, during which we were exposed to a keen north-east wind. An old shirt was all that covered me; I suffered much from the cold; and, in this extremity, M. Langlade coming down to the beach, I asked him for a blanket, promising, if I lived, to pay him for it, at any price he pleased; but, the answer I received was this, that he could let me have no blanket, unless there were someone to be security for the payment. For myself, he observed, I had no longer any property in that country. I had no more to say to M. Langlade; but, presently, seeing another Canadian, named John Cuchoise, I addressed to him a similar request, and was not refused. Naked, as I was, and rigorous as was the weather, but for the blanket, I must have perished. At noon, our party was all collected, the prisoners all embarked, and we steered for the Isles du Castor, in Lake Michigan.

CHAPTER SEVEN

"The soldier, who was our companion in misfortune, was made fast to the bar of the canoe, by a rope tied round his neck, as is the manner of the Indians, in transporting their prisoners. The rest were unconfined; but a paddle was put into each of our hands, and we were made to use it. The Indians in the canoe were seven in number; the prisoners four. I had left, as it will be recollected, Major Etherington, Lieutenant Leslie and Mr. Bostwick, at M. Langlade's, and was now joined in misery with Mr. Ezekiel Solomons, the soldier, and the Englishman who had newly arrived from Detroit. This was on the sixth day of June. The fort was taken on the fourth; I surrendered myself to Wenniway on the fifth; and this was the third day of our distress.

"We were bound, as I have said, for the Isles du Castor, which lie in the mouth of Lake Michigan; and we should have crossed the lake, but that a thick fog came on, on account of which the Indians deemed it safer to keep the shore close under their lee. We therefore approached the lands of the Ottawas, and their village of L'Arbre Croche, already mentioned as lying about twenty miles to the westward of Michilimackinac, on the opposite side of the tongue of land on which the fort is built.

"Every half hour, the Indians gave their warwhoops, one for every prisoner in their canoe. This

Indian tepee inside restored fort at Mackinaw City.

is a general custom, by the aid of which all other Indians, within hearing, are apprized of the number of prisoners they are carrying.

"In this manner, we reached Wagoshense, a long point stretching westward into the lake, and which the Ottawas make a carrying place, to avoid going round it.   It is distant eighteen miles from Michilimackinac.   After the Indians had made their war-whoop, as before, an Ottawa appeared upon the beach, who made signs that we should land.   In consequence, we approached.   The Ottawa asked the news, and kept the Chipeways in further conversation, till we were within a few yards of the land, and in shallow water.   At this moment, a hundred men rushed upon us, from among the bushes, and dragged all the prisoners out of the canoes, amid a terrifying shout.

"We now believed that our last sufferings were approaching; but, no sooner were we fairly on shore, and on our legs, than the chiefs of the party advanced, and gave each of us their hands, telling us that they were our friends, and Ottawas, whom the Chipeways had insulted, by destroying the English without consulting with them on the affair. They added, that what they had done was for the purpose of saving our lives, the Chipeways having been carrying us to the Isles du Castor only to kill and devour us.

"The reader's imagination is here distracted by the variety of our fortunes, and he may well paint to himself the state of mind of those who sustained them; who were the sport, or the victims, of a series of events, more like dreams than realities, more like fiction than truth! It was not long before we were embarked again, in the canoes of the Ottawas, who, the same evening, relanded us at Michilimackinac, where they marched us into the fort, in view of the Chipeways, confounded at beholding the Ottawas espouse a side opposite to their own.

"The Ottawas, who had accompanied us in sufficient numbers, took possession of the fort. We, who had changed masters, but were still prisoners, were lodged in the house of the commandant, and strictly guarded.

"Early the next morning, a general council was held, in which the Chipeways complained much of the conduct of the Ottawas, in robbing them of their prisoners; alleging that all the Indians, the Ottawas alone excepted, were at war with the English; that Pontiac had taken Detroit; that the King of France had awoke, and repossessed himself of Quebec and Montreal; and that the English were meeting destruction, not only at Michilimackinac, but in every other part of the world. From all this they inferred, that it became the Ottawas to restore the prisoners, and to join in the war; and the speech was followed by large presents, being part of the plunder of the fort, and which was previously heaped in the centre of the room. The Indians rarely make their answers till the day after they have heard the arguments offered. They did not depart from their custom on this occasion; and the council therefore adjourned.

"We, the prisoners, whose fate was thus in controversy, were unacquainted at the time, with this transaction; and therefore enjoyed a night of toler-

able tranquility, not in the least suspecting the reverse which was preparing for us.   Which of the
arguments of the Chipeways, or whether or not
all were deemed valid by the Ottawas, I cannot
say; but the council was resumed at an early hour in
the morning, and, after several speeches had been
made in it, the prisoners were sent for, and returned
to the Chipeways.

"The Ottawas, who now gave us into the hands
of the Chipeways, had themselves declared, that
the latter designed no other than to kill us, and
make broth of us.   The Chipeways, as soon as we
were restored to them, marched us to a village of
their own, situate on the point which is below the
fort, and put us into a lodge, already the prison of
fourteen soldiers, tied two and two, with each a
rope about his neck, and made fast to a pole
which might be called the supporter of the building.

"I was left untied; but I passed a night sleepless
and full of wretchedness.   The bed was the bare
ground, and I was again reduced to an old shirt, as
my entire apparel; the blanket which I had received, through the generosity of M. Cuchoise, having
been taken from me among the Ottawas, when they
seized upon myself and the others, at Wagoshense.
I was, besides, in want of food, having for two
days, ate nothing.

"I confess that in the canoe, with the Chipeways, I was offered bread—but, bread, with what
accompaniment!   They had a loaf, which they cut
with the same knives that they had employed in
the massacre—knives still covered with blood.
The blood they moistened with spittle, and rubbing

this on the bread, offered this for food to their
prisoners, telling them to eat the blood of their
countrymen.

"Such was my situation, on the morning of the
seventh of June, in the year one thousand seven
hundred and sixty-three; but a few hours produced
an event which gave still a new color to my lot.

"Toward noon, when the great war-chief, in
company with Wenniway, was seated at the opposite end of the lodge, my friend and brother, Wawatam, suddenly came in. During the four days
preceding, I had often wondered what had become
of him. In passing by, he gave me his hand, but
went immediately toward the great chief, by the
side of whom and Wenniway, he sat himself down.
The most uninterrupted silence prevailed; each
smoked his pipe, and this done, Wawatam arose,
and left the lodge, saying, to me, as he passed,
'Take courage!'

"An hour elapsed, during which several chiefs
entered and preparations appeared to be making
for a council. At length, Wawatam re-entered the
lodge, followed by his wife, and both loaded with
merchandise, which they carried up to the chiefs,
and laid in a heap before them. Some moments of
silence followed, at the end of which Wawatam
pronounced a speech, every word of which, to me,
was of extraordinary interest:

" 'Friends and relations,' he began, 'what is it
that I shall say? You know what I feel. You all
have friends and brothers and children, whom as
yourselves you love; and you—what would you experience, did you, like me, behold your dearest

friend—your brother—in the condition of a slave; a slave, exposed every moment to insult, and to menaces of death? This case, as you all know, is mine. See there' (pointing to myself) 'my friend and brother among slaves—himself a slave!

" 'You all well know, that long before the war began, I adopted him as my brother. From that moment, he became one of my family, so that no change of circumstances could break the cord which fastened us together.

" 'He is my brother, and, because I am your relation, he is therefore your relation too;—and how, being your relation, can he be your slave?

" 'On the day on which the war began, you were fearful, lest, on this very account, I should reveal your secret. You requested, therefore, that I would leave the fort, and even cross the lake. I did so; but I did it with reluctance, notwithstanding that you, Menehwehna, who had the command in this enterprise, gave me your promise that you would protect my friend, delivering him from all danger and giving him safely to me.

" 'The performance of this promise, I now claim. I come not with empty hands to ask it. You, Menehwehna, best know, whether or not, as it respects yourself, you have kept your word, but I bring these goods, to buy off every claim which any man among you all may have on my brother, as his prisoner.'

"Wawatam having ceased, the pipes were again filled; and, after they were finished, a further period of silence followed. At the end of this, Menehwehna arose, and gave his reply:

" 'My relation and brother,' said he, 'what you have spoken is the truth. We were acquainted with the friendship which subsisted between yourself and the Englishman, in whose behalf you have now addressed us. We knew the danger of having our secret discovered, and the consequences which must follow; and you say truly, that we requested you to leave the fort. This we did, out of regard for you and your family; for, if a discovery of our design had been made, you would have been blamed, whether guilty or not; and you would thus have been involved in difficulties from which you could not have extricated yourself.

" 'It is also true, that I promised you to take care of your friend; and this promise I performed, by desiring my son, at the moment of assault, to seek him out, and bring him to my lodge. He went accordingly, but could not find him. The day after, I sent him to Langlade's, when he was informed that your friend was safe; and had it not been that the Indians were then drinking the rum which had been found in the fort, he would have brought him home with him, according to my orders.

" 'I am very glad to find that your friend has escaped. We accept your present; and you may take him home with you.'

"Wawatam thanked the assembled chiefs, and taking me by the hand, led me to his lodge, which was at the distance of a few yards only from the prison lodge. My entrance appeared to give joy to the whole family; food was immediately prepared for me; and I now ate the first hearty meal which I had made since my capture. I found myself one of the family; and but that I had still my fears, as to the other Indians, I felt as happy as the situation could allow.

"In the course of the next morning, I was alarmed by a noise in the prison-lodge; and looking through the openings of the lodge in which I was, I saw seven dead bodies of white men dragged forth. Upon my inquiry into the occasion, I was informed that a certain chief, called, by the Canadians, Le Grand Sable, had not long before arrived from his winter's hunt; and that he, having been absent when the war begun, and being now desirous of manifesting to the Indians at large, his hearty concurrence in what they had done, had gone into the prison-lodge, and there, with his knife, put the seven men, whose bodies I had seen, to death.

"Shortly after, two of the Indians took one of the dead bodies, which they chose as being the fattest, cut off the head, and divided the whole into five parts, one of which was put into each of five kettles, hung over as many fires kindled for this purpose, at the door of the prison-lodge. Soon after things were so far prepared, a message came to our lodge, with an invitation to Wawatam, to assist at the feast.

"An invitation to a feast is given by him who is the master of it. Small cuttings of cedar-wood, of about four inches in length, supply the place of cards; and the bearer, by word of mouth, states the particulars.

"Wawatam obeyed the summons, taking with him, as is usual, to the place of entertainment, his dish and spoon.

"After an absence of about half an hour, he returned, bringing in his dish a human hand, and a large piece of flesh. He did not appear to relish the repast, but told me that it was then, and always had been the custom, among all the Indian nations, when returning from war, or on overcoming their enemies, to make a war-feast, from among the slain. This, he said, inspired the warrior with courage in attack, and bred him to meet death with fearlessness.

"In the evening of the same day, a large canoe, such as those which came from Montreal, was seen advancing to the fort. It was full of men, and I distinguished several passengers. The Indian cry was made in the village; a general muster ordered; and, to the number of two hundred, they marched up to the fort, where the canoe was expected to land. The canoe, suspecting nothing, came boldly to the fort, where the passengers, as being English traders, were seized, dragged through the water, beat, reviled, marched to the prison-lodge, and there stripped of their clothes, and confined.

"Of the English traders that fell into the hands of the Indians, at the capture of the fort, Mr. Tracy was the only one who lost his life. Ezekiel Solomons and Mr. Henry Bostwick were taken by the Ottawas, and, after the peace, carried down to Montreal, and there ransomed. Of ninety troops, about seventy were killed; the rest, together with those of the posts in the Bay des Puants, and at the River Saint-Joseph, were also kept in safety by the Ottawas, till the peace, and then either freely restored, or ransomed at Montreal. The Ottawas never overcame their disgust at the neglect with which they had been treated, in the beginning of the war, by those who afterward desired their assistance as allies.

CHAPTER EIGHT

"In the morning of the ninth of June, a general council was held, at which it was agreed to remove to the Island of Michilimackinac, as a more defensible situation, in the event of an attack by the English. The Indians had begun to entertain apprehensions of want of strength. No news had reached them from the Potawatomies, in the Bay des Puants; and they were uncertain whether or not the Monominis would join them. They even feared that the Sioux would take the English side.

"This resolution fixed, they prepared for a speedy retreat. At noon, the camp was broken up, and we embarked, taking with us the prisoners that were still undisposed of. On our passage, we encountered a gale of wind, and there were some appearances of danger. To avert it, a dog, of which the legs were previously tied together, was thrown into the lake; an offering designed to soothe the angry passions of some offended Ma'ni'to'.

"As we approached the Island, two women, in the canoe in which I was, began to utter melancholy and hideous cries. Precarious as my condition still remained, I experienced some sensations of alarm, from these dismal sounds, of which I could not then discover the occasion. Subsequently, I learned that it is customary for the women, on passing near the burial-places of relations, never to omit the practice of which I was now a witness, and by which they intend to denote their grief.

"By the approach of evening, we reached the island in safety, and the women were not long in erecting our cabins. In the morning, there was a muster of the Indians, at which there were found three hundred and fifty fighting-men.

"In the course of the day, there arrived a canoe from Detroit, with ambassadors, who endeavored to prevail on the Indians to repair thither, to the assistance of Pontiac; but fear was now the prevailing passion. A guard was kept during the day, and alarms were very frequently spread. Had an enemy appeared, all the prisoners would have been put to death; and I suspected, that as an Englishman, I should share their fate.

"Several days had now passed, when, one morning, a continued alarm prevailed, and I saw the Indians running, in a confused manner, toward the beach. In a short time, I learned that two large canoes, from Montreal, were in sight.

"All the Indian canoes were immediately manned, and those from Montreal were surrounded and seized, as they turned a point, behind which the flotilla had been concealed. The goods were consigned to a Mr. Levy, and would have been saved, if the canoe-men had called them French property; but they were terrified, and disguised nothing.

"In the canoes was a large proportion of liquor, a dangerous acquisition, and which threatened disturbance among the Indians, even to the loss of their dearest friends. Wawatam, always watchful of my safety, no sooner heard the noise of drunkenness, which, in the evening did not fail to begin, than he represented to me the danger of remaining

Preparing the "pipe of peace."

in the village, and owned that he could not himself resist the temptation of joining his comrades in the debauch. That I might escape all mischief, he therefore requested that I would accompany him to the mountain, where I was to remain hidden, till the liquor should be drank.

"We ascended the mountain accordingly. It is this mountain which constitutes that high land, in the middle of the island, of which I have spoken before, as of a figure considered as resembling a turtle, and therefore called Michilimackinac. It is thickly covered with wood, and very rocky toward the top. After walking more than half a mile, we came to a large rock, at the base of which was an opening, dark within, and appearing to be the entrance of a cave.

"Here Wawatam recommended that I should take up my lodging, and by all means remain till he returned.

"On going into the cave, of which the entrance was nearly ten feet wide, I found the further end to be rounded in its shape, like that of an oven, but with a further aperture, too small, however, to be explored.

"After thus looking around me, I broke small branches from the trees, and spread them for a bed; then wrapped myself in my blanket, and slept till day-break.

"On awakening, I felt myself incommoded by some object, upon which I lay; and, removing it, found it to be a bone. This I supposed to be that of a deer, or some other animal, and what might very naturally be looked for, in the place in which

I was; but, when day-light visited my chamber, I discovered, with some feelings of horror, that I was lying on nothing less than a heap of human bones, and skulls, which covered all the floor!

"The day passed without the return of Wawatam, and without food. As night approached, I found myself unable to meet its darkness in the charnel-house, which, nevertheless, I had viewed free from uneasiness during the day. I chose, therefore, an adjacent bush for this night's lodging, and slept under it as before; but, in the morning, I awoke hungry and dispirited, and almost envying the dry bones, to the view of which I returned. At length, the sound of a foot reached me, and my Indian friend appeared, making many apologies for his long absence, the cause of which was an unfortunate excess in the enjoyment of his liquor.

"This point being explained, I mentioned the extraordinary sight that had presented itself, in the cave to which he had commended my slumbers. He had never heard of its existence before; and, upon examining the cave together, we saw reason to believe that it had been anciently filled with human bodies.

"On returning to the lodge, I experienced a cordial reception from the family, which consisted of the wife of my friend, his two sons, of whom the eldest was married, and whose wife, and daughter, of thirteen years of age, completed the list.

"Wawatam related to the other Indians the adventure of the bones. All of them expressed surprise at hearing it, and declared that they had never been aware of the contents of this cave before.

After visiting it, which they immediately did, almost every one offered a different opinion, as to its history.

"Some advanced, that at a period when the waters overflowed the land (an event which makes a distinguished figure in the history of their world), the inhabitants of this island had fled into the cave, and been there drowned; others, that those same inhabitants, when the Hurons made war upon them (as tradition says they did), hid themselves in the cave, and being discovered, were there massacred. For myself, I am disposed to believe, that this cave was an ancient receptacle of the bones of prisoners, sacrificed and devoured at war-feasts. I have always observed, that the Indians pay particular attention to the bones of sacrifices, preserving them unbroken, and depositing them in some place kept exclusively for that purpose."

According to Henry's account, a few days after this the chief Minavavana came to the lodge of his friend, and warning Henry of the approach of hostile Indians assisted him to escape in the disguise of an Indian. In this disguise he visited the fort, succeeded in finding his French clerks, but could recover none of his goods. Abandoning his trading plans, he visited St. Martin's Island, and later in company with Wawatam spent the winter in hunting. In the spring he returned to Mackinaw, where he found only two French traders and a few Indians. His winter's hunting had netted him about $160. There he learned that a band of Indians from Saginaw Bay were approaching, and was informed by some who arrived in advance that they proposed to kill him "in order to give their friends a mess of English broth, to raise their courage."

An opportunity presented itself to reach Sault Ste. Marie, in company with Madame Cadotte, the Chippewa wife of a Sault trader, who was returning from Montreal. This was at the Isle aux Outardes, whither Henry, with Wawatam and his family had gone for safety, and it was there that Henry parted with his friends.

"We now exchanged farewells," he says, "with an emotion entirely reciprocal. I did not quit the lodge without the most grateful sense of the many acts of goodness which I had experienced in it, nor without the sincerest respect for the virtues which I had witnessed among its members. All the family accompanied me to the beach; and the canoe had no sooner put off, than Wawatam commenced an address to the Ki'chi' Ma'ni'to', beseeching him to take care of me, his brother, till we should next meet. This, he had told me, would not be long, as he intended to return to Michilimackinac for a short time only, and would then follow me to the Sault. We had proceeded to too great a distance to allow of our hearing his voice, before Wawatam had ceased to offer up his prayers."

The next day Henry arrived at the Sault, but hostile Indians were there from Mackinaw inquiring for him and he was compelled to take refuge in a garret. On learning that he was under the protection of M. Cadotte, who assured them that Henry was now under the immediate protection of all the chiefs, they desisted from their purpose. Soon after this a deputation arrived from Sir William Johnson, inviting the Indians to Niagara to partake of a great feast, in common with the Six Nations of the Iroquois, which had all made peace with the English; and the invitation was reinforced with the assurance that unless they complied, the English before the fall of the leaf, would be at Michilimackinac and the Six Nations with them. The return of the deputation with the northern Indians offered Henry the means of leaving the country.

"Very little time was proposed to be lost in setting forward on the voyage," says Henry, "but the occasion was of too much magnitude not to call for more than human knowledge and discretion; and preparations were accordingly made for solemnly invoking and consulting the Great Turtle."

In due course Henry, accompanying the deputation of Indians, arrived at Niagara safe, delivered finally from the grave dangers which trading at Mackinaw had brought down upon the head of an Englishman.

CHAPTER NINE

For a year following the massacre Old Mackinaw was occupied only by a few French traders, while the deserted fort remained without even a sentry. But Sir William Johnson, colonial English frontier leader, lost no time in making peace with his far flung Indian foes, and a council at Niagara was followed by the re-occupation of Fort Michilimackinac in August, 1764, by two companies of English regulars and an artillery force under Capt. William Howard. Historians are again in dispute as to whether a new fort was erected at this time at Old Mackinaw or the fort which was the scene of the Pontiac massacre restored and re-occupied. This writer is one of those who believe that no new fort was constructed. Be that as it may, the site of Fort Michilimackinac has never been changed since it was first built by the French commandant, de Louvigny.

Described by Sir William Johnson at that time as "the most material post we have", Old Mackinaw and its fort went through the next thirteen years with the usual military and trading routine, including the annual gathering and departure of the fur traders and their Indian hunters, but without any serious disturbances beyond those within the fort itself.

Early in this period, in 1765, the noted ranger, Major Robert Rogers (hero of Kenneth Roberts' best selling 1937 book, "Northwest Passage") became commandant at Fort Michilimackinac. Rogers, realizing his distance from English headquarters, is alleged to have turned the trading in furs at Mackinaw to his personal advantage. In a single year he drew on Sir William Johnson for the immense sum, in those days, of $25,000, and greatly resented the arrival of an officer from Niagara to check upon his expenditures.

Had secret plans of Major Rogers not been interrupted by the investigation of his commanding officer, Sir William Johnson, another stirring tragedy might have entered the annals of Fort Michilimackinac. It had been rumored throughout this section of the Northwest that Rogers, with one or two confederates, had a well laid plan to sack and abandon the old mainland fort and to enlist with the French in the Mississippi country, presumably with the idea of a concerted effort to win back for France this Northwest territory, acquired by the British with the surrender of Montcalm at Quebec.

Rogers was heavily in debt, and hard pressed for payment of the several hundred thousand livres he owed to traders and merchants. He was also intensely ambitious, and visualized himself as the new governor of the territory, should the French win it back.

Incidental to the Rogers regime at Fort Michilimackinac is a statement which is part of the controversy as to what became of the original fort after the Pontiac massacre in 1763, four years before the bristling Rogers took command. The editor of Rogers' "Ponteach" tells us that the fort was "newly built since Pontiac's war (on, however, the original site) but was not a prepossessing structure, for it was neither commodious nor strong. Heavy barracks rose near the fort proper, and at some distance stood the French village of Mackinaw". Other authorities, however, hold that "newly built" meant only repairs necessary after the Pontiac raid.

Major Rogers had brought with him to Mackinaw full powers as commandant and Indian agent. His practical isolation from all headquarters control offered a constant temptation to indulge in schemes to advance his private gain, in the fur trade and in general trading with the Red men. His colleague in various adventurous schemes was Jonathan Carver, a Connecticut Yankee who had served as an officer with the British army at the battle of Lake George. Together Rogers and Carver planned, and even commenced, a search for the mythical "Northwest Passage", which made a feeble ending in a dispute between the two as to who originated the plan, and a contest with the British government over the payment of its expenses.

When Sir William Johnson, angered by Rogers' disregard of orders, his large drafts for money, his dissipation and accumulating debts, together with alarming reports of the condition of affairs at Fort Michilimackinac, ordered Benjamin Roberts, commissary at Niagara, to journey north and make a thorough investigation, Major Rogers was bold enough to submit to London a plan which would have eliminated Sir William's control by drafting a new and independent government for Mackinaw with Rogers as governor. A student of the ill

fated Rogers' regime, Allan Nevins of Chicago, in
his able book on the subject, tells us that: "It was
clear that Rogers, under a scheme for promoting
trade, was virtually proposing that he be given the
most absolute control over the Indian tribes, the
fur business, the garrison of the Northwest and a
large sum of money."

Quite naturally Benjamin Roberts received a
chilly reception from the commandant on his arrival
at Fort Michilimackinac. He was hampered greatly
in his investigations. Roberts promptly reported to
Sir William the evidences he found of mismanage-
ment and the illicit schemes of Rogers' for his personal benefit, describing the general Mackinaw
personnel as "simple, canting, over-reaching New
Englanders who watch every opportunity of making
the Indians drunk, cheating them of their furs, and
continually abusing one another".

Meantime Rogers' secretary, one Potter, had
returned from what Roberts believed to be a
traitorous mission in the Lake Superior section.
The commandant and his messenger presently
came to blows, and Rogers locked Potter in the
guard house. The secretary, in revenge or through
repentance, made a clean breast of the unborn conspiracy to Roberts, telling him that Rogers had
determined a full month before that, if his plans
for an independent government of Mackinaw were
not approved by England, he would close at once
with an offer he (Rogers) had received from the
French, which included the desertion of those
soldiers who might be persuaded to join him, the
rifling of the trading posts along the lakes and a

"full handed" joining with the French west of the Illinois country. Potter said his refusal to take part had led to his open fight with Rogers, who had threatened him with instant death if he revealed the plan.

Promptly orders came from Sir William for the arrest of Rogers, and he was sent to Niagara in chains. Shortly he was tried at Montreal for mutiny, but acquitted, through the influence of his creditors, who hoped that if freed they might collect the money due them. The innocent investigator, Benjamin Roberts, was arrested in some effort at revenge, but promptly acquitted. Thus ended what might well have been another tragedy at Fort Michilimackinac, changing the whole subsequent history of the Northwest territory and the Straits of Mackinac section.

When the War of the Revolution broke out in 1776 Major A. S. De Peyster was in command of the English forces at Fort Michilimackinac and its dependencies. In 1778 he was greatly disturbed by continued reports that the Americans were planning the capture of Detroit and all British posts on the northern lakes. On August 31, 1778, De Peyster wrote to General Haldimand, the English governor: "I am informed that the rebels are in possession of all the Illinois. The traders in that country and many from this post have been plundered. The whole country is in the greatest confusion, being at a loss to know which route the rebels will take next." He regretted his not having ships on the northern lakes, wondered whether he might rely on the Indians for assistance, and added: "If

Detroit should be taken we have but a dismal prospect."

De Peyster took strenuous steps to strengthen the stockades around Fort Michilimackinac. He had a fairly strong garrison, but realized that if Detroit, his base of supplies, should fall his own post was sure to be lost.

In October, 1779, De Peyser was succeeded by Captain Patrick Sinclair, named as "Lieutenant Governor and Superintendent of Indian Affairs" in addition to his command at Old Mackinaw. Sinclair came by boat from Detroit, stopping en route at Mackinac Island. At once he compared the Island with the mainland for military and defense purposes. He promptly decided, with hearty approval from De Peyster, that Mackinac Island offered a "respectable and convenient situation for a Fort".

The retiring and incoming commandants of Fort Michilimackinac at Mackinaw City lost no time in advising General Haldimand of the wisdom of moving their defenses to Mackinac Island. After a few weeks of reconnoitering and study these officers wrote the requiem of the fort at Mackinaw City to their superior as follows: "This place (Old Mackinaw) being defenseless, and all our dependence on fish, we would be entirely cut off. We are certainly liable to be attacked from Lake Michigan, and this may be very justly looked upon as the object of a second expedition of the Rebels."

The story of the evacuation of the English mainland fort on the Straits of Mackinac is told in the pages which follow. Suffice it to say here that the old mainland stockade fell into decay, withered and died. Time, weather and neglect razed the pickets and the log buildings, and as a century rolled around the site became an abandoned lakeside field.

In 1909 the Mackinaw City bay shore, which had been used as a park by the little village, was ceded to the State of Michigan as a state park, under the jurisdiction of the State Park commission which now has supervision of the old fort on Mackinac Island.

In 1922 Chris Schneider, son of a German Army surgeon who had located in Cross Village, on the Straits of Mackinac, for relief from asthma and hay fever, was named as custodian of the Mackinaw City State park. Mr. Schneider had been raised among the Indians, speaks many of their dialects fluently and is well posted on the history of this famous section.

Year after year he continued to unearth arrow heads and hatchets, pewter spoons and household utensils, barrels of guns, the wood work of which had long ago crumbled. He urged the reconstruction of the old fort, and in 1931 the legislature of Michigan gave the Mackinac Island State Park Commission sufficient funds for this purpose. Records in the British museum were made available and surveys carefully prepared. The final excavations disclosed the absolute accuracy of the location, revealing the rotting timbers of the old stockade and a host of buried relics of its military, Indian and domestic occupation. Exactly on the same spot, exactly along the same lines, exactly of the

same construction as at the time of the Pontiac massacre in 1763, restored Old Fort Michilimackinac
stands today in the State park at Mackinaw City.

Within its historic gates is maintained in summer an Indian village and an historical museum
containing a thrilling collection of the relics of
nearly two hundred years ago.   More than one
hundred and fifty thousand visitors annually make
their summer trek to this Michigan State park on
the shores of the Straits of Mackinac, enjoying one
of America's finest rustic groves, one of America's
best appointed and maintained auto and trailer
camps, and freedom from hay fever, excessive heat
and the turmoil of the city.   Remaining as their
friendly and enthusiastic host is Custodian Chris
Schneider, affectionately and widely known to
young and old as "The Buffalo Bill of the Mackinac
country."

BRITISH COMMANDANTS OF FORT MICHILIMACKINAC AT MACKINAW CITY AND FORT MACKINAC AT MACKINAC ISLAND

Mackinaw City

1761—Major George Etherington.

1765—Major Robert Rogers.

1774—Major A. S. De Peyster.

1779—Major and Lieut. Governor Patrick Sinclair.

Mackinac Island

1780—Major and Lieut. Governor Patrick Sinclair.

1782—Capt. Daniel Robertson.

1784—Lieut. George Clowes.

1791—Capt. Edward Charleton.

1795—Captain Doyle.

1812—Capt. Charles Roberts.

1814—Lieut. Col. Robert McDouall.

Entrance to Michilimackinac State Park at
Mackinaw City, Michigan.

OLD FORT MACKINAC
ON THE HILL OF HISTORY
At Mackinac Island

CHAPTER ONE

The American Revolution, begun in 1776, had been under way for three eventful years when Captain Patrick Sinclair of the British army, was assigned by General Haldimand, the British governor of the Northwest territory, to command Fort Michilimackinac at Old Mackinaw.

Even before the departure of his predecessor commandant, DePeyster, Captain Sinclair had received tentative approval of their joint recommendation that Fort Michilimackinac be removed from Mackinaw City on the mainland to Mackinac Island. The accomplishment of this removal was the most important development of the Revolutionary war in the Straits of Mackinac territory.

There is little doubt that these British officers urged this change of base for two reasons; first, fear of the Indians who had remained hostile to the English control; and, second, because of the success of the American arms under George Rogers Clark in the Ohio valley, where the Virginian had courageously defended the American frontier settlements from the British, and particularly from the atrocities of the "hair buying" English General Hamilton and his paid Iroquois, operating out of the fort at Detroit. When the news reached Mackinaw that General Hamilton had been captured and sent east in irons by the Americans, consternation struck the little garrison of Fort Michilimackinac. The old fort was at once repaired and strengthened wherever possible and efforts made to insure the help, in case of attack, of the few Indians who were friendly to the British cause. Captain Sinclair reported to headquarters that "if we were to be attacked by any considerable force Mackinac Island would be our place of greatest safety".

Workmen were sent over to Mackinac Island to study its topography, and they reported the advantageous location of the "Hill of History", rising nearly two hundred feet above the lake level, and offering a broad defensive coverage of the Straits. Again reporting to General Haldimand, Sinclair wrote: "Mackinac Island offers (for defense) the most respectable situation I ever saw, besides convenient for the subsistence of a garrison, the safety of troops, traders and commerce". He contrasted the new location with the "defenseless" one on the mainland, clinching his argument with the statement that "on Mackinac Island there is an abundance of stone easily raised and cut or shaped at pleasure. . . . The upper ground for officers' and soldiers' barracks, powder magazines and provision store house, and the lower part (of the Island) for traders and the person who manages the Indians."

However, the Island was the occupied property of the Indians, and it was certainly unwise to strain their indifferent attitude toward the British King by seizing it by force. After much negotiation a treaty was made with four important Indian chiefs, under the terms of which they sold "forever the Island of Michilimackinac, or, as it is called by the Canadians 'La Grosse Isle' ", to King George the Third of England for the cash sum of five thousand pounds ($25,000). A perfect replica of this famous bill of sale, on exhibition today in the museum at Fort Mackinac, acknowledged by the chiefs with their marks, reads as follows:

* * *

DEED TO THE ISLAND OF MICHILIMAKINAK

May 12th, 1781

CHIPPEWA INDIANS TO GEORGE III

By these presents, we the following Chiefs Kitch Negou or Grand Sable Powanas, Keusse & Magousseigan in behalf of ourselves & all others of our nation, the Chipwas, who have or can lay claim to ye herein mentioned island, as being their representatives and chiefs by & with mutual consent do surrender & yield up into the hands of Lieutenant Governour Sinclair, for the behalf and use of His Majesty George III of Great Britain, France and Ireland, King, Defender of the Faith, etc., etc., his heirs, executors, administrators forever, the Island of Michilimakinak or as its called by the Canadians, La Grosse Island (situate at that Strait which joins the Lakes Huron & Michigan) & we do hereby make for ourselves in posterity a renunciation of all claims in future to said island.

We also acknowledge to have received, by command of His Excellency Frederick Haldimand, Esquire, Governour of the Province of Quebec, General and Commander in Chief of all His Majesty's forces in Canada, etc., etc., from the said Lieutenant Governour Sinclair on His Majesty's behalf, the sum of Five Thousand Pounds New York currency being the adequate & compleat value of the before mentioned island of Michilimakinak & have signed the deeds of this tenor & date.

We promise to preserve in our village a belt of wampum of seven feet in length to perpetuate, secure & be a lasting memorial of the said transaction to our Nation forever & hereafter, & that no defect in this deed from want of law forms or any other shall invalidate the same.

In witness whereof we the above mentioned chiefs do set our hands & seals this Twelfth day of May in the year of our Lord Seventeen Hundred & Eighty One, & the Twenty First year of His Majesty's reign.

* * *

This document was executed with the totems and seals of the four Indian Chiefs named in the first paragraph of the deed, and was signed for King George by Lieutenant Governor and Commandant "Patt" Sinclair, Captain John Mompesson and Lieutenant R. B. Brooke, officers of the King's Eighth Regiment, together with Ensign John Robert McDougall.

In a diplomatic acknowledgement of the approval of General Haldimand of the plans for establishing the new fort on Mackinac Island, Sinclair named the curving harbor on the south side "Haldimand Bay", and in the winter of 1780, while the ice offered an easy method of transport from the mainland, the work of removal was begun. The site of the Island fort had been cleared to the extent of four acres, and a harbor wharf constructed some 150 feet out from shore into a depth of two fathoms, providing the dockage which the mainland fort and village had lacked. At the same time a block house, now standing at the west side of Fort

Mackinac, was constructed as emergency protection for the new work of occupation and construction.

First building to be removed from Mackinaw to Mackinac was the old Catholic church, located in the lower village, so that "the worship and work of the Canadians will be drawn to the Island next year". Difficulties of transportation and the tearing down and re-erection of buildings, however primitive in construction, greatly delayed the work of transfer and completion of the fortifications. Meantime a cautious eye was kept against possible hostile demonstrations by the Indians or the approach of any Continental forces from the south. However, no threat developed from either enemy source.

Projects begun in 1780 moved slowly through that summer, and into the winter of 1781. By July of that year, however, Sinclair was able to report that his men "had raised the old provision store; the soldiers' barracks, with stone chimneys; the powder magazine; and have kept raising the defenses of the fort. All the troops and stores will be within the works by October (1781). One half of the garrison is now here, with provisions for one year for 100 men." At this time the British not only were in possession of the fort at Detroit, but also based at that point what they were pleased to call "The Naval Armament on the Rivers and Lakes of Canada". One of these vessels, the sloop "Welcome", greatly aided Sinclair in the evacuation of the fort at Mackinaw City, first carrying supplies and timbers from the mainland, and later bringing new soldiers from Detroit.

The three years which intervened between the establishment of Fort Mackinac by the British in 1780, and the winning of the Revolutionary war by the Americans, culminating in the treaty of Paris in 1783, were spent by Sinclair and succeeding officers in efforts to speed the entire completion of their Island fortress. That they were unable to completely finish their task is evidenced by their reports from time to time and their repeated requisitions for more supplies. Eventually Captain Sinclair fell into disfavor with General Haldimand, largely because of heavy expenditures which the latter insisted were unnecessary, and in 1782 the command of the new fort was turned over to Captain Daniel Robertson.

Long drawn out disputes regarding the Canadian border line kept Fort Mackinac under the British flag for thirteen years after the treaty of Paris. During that time its Island defense development moved slowly, because of the uncertainty as to its ownership. Naturally the English, waiting to see whether their title would survive the territorial negotiations, were reluctant to expend time and money in further building. Captain Robertson was succeeded as commandant in 1784 by Lieut. George Clowes, followed in 1791 by Captain Edward Charleton, who remained until October, 1796, when he hauled down the English flag and turned Fort Mackinac over to Major Henry Burbeck, the first American commander. This transfer was the final incident of the Revolutionary war.

Major Burbeck hastened to bring to completion the defenses of the Island fort. The English upon

Airplane view of Fort Mackinac today.

leaving had established a post, commanded by
Captain Doyle, on St. Joseph's Island, only 40
miles east of Mackinac Island, near the outlet of
the St. Mary's river, and the officers at Fort Mackinac, with this fact in mind, determined that pru-
dence was the better part of valor.

With all possible speed the American occupation finished the protective enclosures of Fort
Mackinac. Its surrounding wall and stockade, as
constructed nearly 140 years ago, stand today with
only slight changes from the original design of part
stone and part pickets. Along its south line at the
exposed brow of the hill, there are the massive
stone wall and ramparts built by Sinclair. These extend the full front length of the fortress, broken
only by the sally port entrance at the end of the
steep path leading up from the base of the stone
wall. Portions of the north, west and east defenses
consist of part masonry, to the height of some fifteen to twenty feet, surmounted by pickets, topped
with five-pronged spikes four inches high, to prevent successful scaling. With but slight repairs,
these solid stone ramparts have stood the ravages
of time and weather, but the original pickets rotted
and were replaced some years ago. The spikes
capping the old pickets were mostly lost down the
years, but replaced by exact duplicates of the first
model, originals of which are on exhibit in the fort
museum.

CHAPTER TWO

Perhaps no better description of Fort Mackinac of yesterdays and today can be given the reader than to undertake a personally conducted visit within its gates.

The Guard House

Entering the fort under the stone archway at the south sally port, once protected by heavy gates and portcullis, and saluting the colors which wave from sun-up to sundown on their tall staff, the first building on our left is the old guard house. Ancient drawings indicate that this building, about 30 feet square, was constructed in 1782. Its stone foundations were laid deep and strong to provide a dungeon for prisoners. The wood superstructure has been several times restored, but always with the iron barred windows of the original. Legend had reported a dungeon somewhere on the fort but it remained for Warren L. Rindge of Grand Rapids, an eminent consulting architect, engaged by the Federal National Park Service to study the structural conditions of Fort Mackinac, to discover in 1933 the almost entirely filled-in stone stairway under the guard house which led to the forbidding dungeon underneath. In the dark recesses workmen found aged clay pipes, with the maker's date of long ago, and on the wall chain fastenings to secure desperate inmates. It was well named the "Black Hole", for cases appear on its record of dead men's bodies be-

ing found. The original crude iron bars on the
doors and windows were hammered into shape by
the fort blacksmith.

The Old Canteen

Just west of the guard house is the old canteen
building, perhaps sixty feet long by thirty feet
wide, its south side containing a long porch which
gives a marvellous marine view of the Straits and
Lakes Huron and Michigan. Among the early
buildings of British construction, the canteen was
first used as officers' quarters. It then consisted of
three apartments, each with a fireplace providing
the only means of both heating and cooking. In
1862 these quarters were occupied by three distinguished Confederate officers, held as prisoners of
war. Today the canteen is one of the two buildings
containing the fort museum, an exceptional collection of exhibits which include Indian arrow heads,
spears and utensils, colonial furniture, arms and ammunition, duelling pistols, military equipment of the
Revolutionary, the Civil and the World wars, the
first Washington hand press to come to Michigan,
and a host of other educational and historical exhibits, maintained free to the public by the Mackinac Island State Park Commission.

Officers Stone Quarters

Directly west of the canteen is "the pride of
the old fort", the Officers Stone Quarters, which
have stood on the brow of the fort hill overlooking
the Straits for 157 years. This building we know

was partly, if not entirely, built by the British under Captain Sinclair. That it is the best preserved of all the fort buildings speaks volumes for the methods and materials of its construction. Describing it Sinclair wrote to General Haldimand: "The upper ground for officers and soldiers barracks would be a safe and easy disposition of the whole garrison". In 1800 an American officer reported to the war department that this building was "equal, if not superior, to any building of its kind in the United States". The exposed north and east sides are surrounded by a deep moat, some four feet in width, which offered additional protection and permitted a mobile defense without exposure to enemy bullets or arrows.

In the year 1919 the basement was remodeled. An opening was cut between the two sets of quarters, both on the first floor and in the basement, not however, without a great deal of difficulty. The old lime mortar had to be chiselled from around each stone and the walls were found to be 26 and 56 inches thick respectively. A quarry tile floor was laid in place of the old wood floor in the east room and the wood floors in the other rooms were renewed. The fireplaces, which had been sealed since before 1878, were opened up in the east and west chimneys. The old andirons and cranes were found intact and were put back in use. It would be interesting to know if the center chimney, which is nearly eight feet thick in the basement, also contains sealed-up fireplaces.

The Stone Quarters is in very good condition. Its masonry is much better preserved than that of the block houses and ramparts. The exterior walls are 25 inches thick above the first floor and 38 inches below. They were evidently intended to be proof against the musketry of the day.

The whole structure has the appearance of solidity and permanence. It is one of the best proportioned buildings comprising the fort group. Its massive stone chimneys with their plastered brick cowls tend to dwarf the scale of the 105 foot building in comparison with the other buildings seen from the parade ground.

Today the old stone building contains the principal museum exhibits referred to in the foregoing description of the canteen. Few, if any, buildings in the traditions of the army of the United States offer a more intriguing appeal to the sight-seer than this solid block of defensive stone on the "Hill of History."

The Beaumont Fort Hospital

At the west end of the hollow square, the parade ground, around which Fort Mackinac buildings stand, is the Beaumont fort hospital, built of logs by the Americans about 1817. It occupies the site of the old provisions store which Captain Sinclair brought over on the ice from Mackinaw City in 1781. Captain Thomas C. Legate, USA, in 1821 converted the building into a hospital, in charge of the post surgeon, the unique and courageous Dr. William Beaumont. The fame of Dr. Beaumont rests largely upon an accident which brought him international renown. An Indian, Alexis St. Martin, was accidentally wounded by the discharge of a shot gun, fired in the stone store at the foot of the

fort hill, operated by the American Fur Company.
The full charge of the gun, including the wadding,
entered the close-up body of St. Martin at the pit of
his stomach. He fell, supposedly dead. Dr. Beaumont was summoned, and gave emergency first aid,
but stated that the man was beyond hope. However, St. Martin remained alive and as soon as he
could be moved was transferred to the fort hospital, where the post surgeon undertook a daring pro-
cess of treatment, resulting in the recovery of the
patient, though the stomach wound did not close
and it was possible from visual observation for Dr.
Beaumont to study those processes of digestion and
the gastric juices which he made public more than
100 years ago, and which still remain, in large part,
a basis of modern medicine and surgery. The physician watched and recorded the phenomena of the
human stomach, and resigned from the army to
give his life to lecturing on his discoveries to medical groups and colleges. A passing comment is
that St. Martin survived his doctor by sixteen years.

Many U. S. Army hospitals throughout the
country are named in honor of Post Surgeon William Beaumont, and some years ago the medical
societies of Michigan, in both peninsulas, joined in
erecting on the grounds of Fort Mackinac a beautiful stone monument to their distinguished fellow.
The inscription there-on reads:

*   *   *

"Near this spot Dr. William Beaumont,
U. S. Army, made the experiments upon
Alexis St. Martin, which brought fame to
himself and honor to American medicine."

The present fort hospital, named for Beaumont, has been, since 1923, taken over, equipped and maintained as a summer hospital, through the generosity of both all year and seasonal residents of Mackinac Island. Each summer it is open as an emergency hospital, in charge of registered nurses, and fully equipped for both surgical and medicinal cases.

The Three Block House.

Directly west of the hospital, forming a section of the rampart wall, is the first block house constructed by the British. It was the only point of protection and defense while the wharf was being constructed in 1780. There are now three ancient block houses on Fort Mackinac and a description of the first will suffice for the two built later on by either the British or the early Americans. These historical block houses are from 18 to 20 feet square, built of solid limestone, two feet thick, for the two lower stories, with a third story of squared logs six inches thick laid horizontally. The hip roofs are framed of heavy squared timbers with sturdy tie beams tennioned in place.

They were intended for defense in case of attack, and so built that such defense might be maintained from the upper two floors, while the women and children were safe in the basement section. Port holes of widening outlet gave a sweeping view to the gunners, and fire places provided for the preparation of food or the giving of heat in case of winter siege. The block houses were occupied by townspeople who were British prisoners of war after

South view, Old Fort Mackinac and Marquette Statue.

the capture of Fort Mackinac in the early days of the War of 1812. Later they contained the British women and children during the American blockade, and after peace was restored they housed the families of the non-commissioned officers. At one time the north block house contained the fort reservoir which had been built into its upper story by an inventive American officer, Major Dwight H. Kelton.

Senior Officers' Quarters.

The two residences at the west end of the fort, and outside its original limits, were built in 1876 as quarters for the senior officers. Their ample rooms offered a new kind of home life to the commanders and their staffs, while their location gave a thrilling view up and down the Straits. The larger residence was occupied in 1877 by the commandant, Major Charles A. Webb, 22nd Infantry, USA, whose widow still lives on Mackinac Island, one of its oldest and most respected citizens. The house nearest the fort enclosure was some years ago designated by the Michigan Legislature as the official "Governor's Cottage", where the state chief executive is in frequent summer residence.

Superintendent's Residence.

Stepping back into the original enclosure we discover the residence, built in 1835, and occupied by the early commandants and their families, together with the company commanders. For a while, in 1842, the west section of the house was the home of the Catholic chaplain of the garrison.

This house is now used as the residence of the Fort superintendent.

Main Flag Staff.

Just below its porch is the main flag staff of the fort. While re-inforcing this staff in 1869 a bottle was discovered in its base containing a parchment on which was written: "This flag staff erected on May 25th, 1835, by A and G companies of United States Infantry stationed here. Commanding officer, Captain John Clitz. Builder of flag staff, Private John McCraith." Another document was added and entombed with the original in the re-built cement foundations. A specific condition of the award of Fort Mackinac by the Federal government to the State of Michigan in 1895 provides that each day of the year the colors shall wave from the fort staff from sunrise to sunset, and this provision has been lived up to without fail for 43 years of state administration.

Fort School House.

Passing the primitive shed which stores the Fort fire hose, a few steps to the east brings us to the old school house, erected in 1878 for the children of the officers and men of the garrison. It was also used as a library and reading room for the enlisted men. In 1895, after the evacuation of the Federal troops, this building was converted into its present use as the office of the fort superintendent and the State Park commission.

The Old Barracks.

A short stairway returns us to the central parade ground and face to face with the old barracks, the largest building on Fort Mackinac. Here Sinclair built his first log quarters for the men of his command. In 1856 a new one story barracks was constructed on the original foundations, to accommodate a single company of fifty soldiers. But in 1875, when Fort Mackinac became a two company post, a second story was added and a long porch built the full length of both floors, facing the parade ground. These quarters provided mess rooms, sleeping wards and kitchens, one company being housed on each floor. Today part of the building has been made into official apartments, but the large center rooms remain as they were in the occupation days. They are used for the display of many historical and development exhibits, and are open to the public.

The "Lost" Well.

Just north of the main sally port entrance, hard by the old guard house, was once located the old fort well. It was sunk deep in the limestone and gave plenty of pure water. For some reason it later became contaminated and was filled in, but the depression of the earth clearly shows its old location. There is a tradition which says that on the morning of the capture of the fort by the British (July 17th, 1812) the American commander, Lieut. Porter Hanks, when he awoke to find the British guns glaring down at him from the hill north of the fort (now the site of the reconstructed Fort Holmes, once Fort George), hastily threw much of his ordnance and side arms into the 80 foot well and had it quickly closed up. This story has some support in the fact that there was a discrepancy of 15 guns (or small field pieces) between the last available ordnance inventory of June, 1794, and the guns found when the British took score of their gains after the capture on July 17, 1812. Some day the State of Michigan will probably finance an excavation to learn the truth.

Close to the old well stands the commissary or supply building, built by the Americans in 1877, on what was the site of Captain Sinclair's first stone powder magazine.

The small buildings to the north have been joined into one, but originally formed the offices of the Commandant and Adjutant of the post and the fort bakery of the early days.

Next north is a small building, its construction date unknown, which was the bath house for the enlisted men. It has been converted into a small administration cottage.

Eagle Scout Barracks.

Ahead of us now is the north sally port of Fort Mackinac, arched like the main entrance and once protected by heavy gates of wood and iron and a portcullis. It opens onto the original farm section of the military reservation, which is now used as an athletic field. Fronting it on the east end is the Eagle Scout Barracks built by the Federal government as a WPA employment project in 1934 to accommodate the Governor's Honor Guard of

Guides and Guards, established in 1929, and to which each summer come merit-selected Michigan Eagle Scouts (the senior rank of Boy Scouts of America) for seasonal service and recreation. No better comment may be made on this Scout service than to say that in nine years more than 500 senior Scouts have been detailed here, rendering first aid, guide duty, emergency service in the Fort fire brigade and helpfulness wherever and whenever called upon. During those years no Scout guide has been absent without leave, received a demerit mark or accepted a tip.

Other Buildings.

Turning back again towards the south we pass a little white cottage, the residence of the assistant superintendent, which was for many years the fort morgue. Beyond this and at the extreme east end of the reservation is a small building, formerly occupied by the post hospital steward, and this adjoins the larger building, which became the fort hospital, or surgeon's post, when the small hospital of the earlier years proved too limited in its capacity. From the full length porches, both on the first and second floors of the surgeon's post, is one of the most commanding marine views in America. The old building has been made into four apartments for State executive use during the summer season.

Nearing the end of our tour of inspection we approach the heaviest part of the rampart masonry, some forty feet of solid stone at the eastern end of the fort wall. Here, as in other locations, are mounted old cannon, attracting constant visitor attention and enhancing the military aspects of Fort Mackinac from as far as it can be seen on incoming vessels. A gradual flight of steps brings us down to the little sentry box over the south sally port, and to the worn sentry "beat" of some fifty feet directly over the main gate. Here British and American soldiers have walked innumerable miles on sentry duty, with a complete view of the fort on one side and on the other an unobstructed outlook over the land and water approaches for twenty miles or more.

So much for a description of old Fort Mackinac on the Hill of History as it stands today.

Sentry duty at Fort Mackinac, 1870.

CHAPTER THREE

On June 19, 1812, war was declared by President Madison between the United States and Great Britain. The Americans had then occupied Fort Mackinac for about 16 years. The commander on the Island was Lieut. Porter Hanks, with a garrison of only 57 effective officers and men. He had kept as fully posted as possible on the events along the Atlantic coast which indicated that once more England and America might resort to arms to settle their disputes. But so remote was Fort Mackinac and so meagre the means of communication with Washington, that actually the commander did not know for a certainty that war had been declared until the fateful morning of July 17, 1812, when the enemy stood nearly twenty to one at his gate. It is significant that General Hull, commander of the American forces at Detroit, did not learn of the new war until fourteen days after its declaration.

It will be recalled that the British upon leaving Mackinac Island in 1796 established an armed post 40 miles to the east on the shores of St. Joseph Island. On the 30th of June, 1812, Captain Charles Roberts had with him at St. Joseph a garrison of about 50 officers and men, together with some artillery equipment. This force was augmented by several hundred Indian allies and some Canadian militia, and on July 8th an express came to the commander from the British General Brock at

York to proceed at once with his combined forces to re-capture Fort Mackinac and the Island.

Lieutenant Hanks learned from a friendly Indian that this attack was believed to be in contemplation by the British, and he immediately summoned a number of American gentlemen residing on the Island to consider what should be done. It was decided to send a reliable scout to St. Joseph Island to observe and report on what was going forward. Michael Dousman, an Island militiaman, was selected for this dangerous errand and started at once in a canoe. Within fifteen miles of the Fort he encountered the oncoming British forces, was himself taken prisoner and put on his parole of honor.

His Majesty's forces, under the command of Captain Charles Roberts of the Tenth Royal Veteran Battalion, consisted of forty-six regulars of the same regiment, with two six-pounders. They had embarked from St. Joseph on board the N. W. Co.'s ship, "Caledonia." Added were two hundred and sixty Canadians, with their employes, and seven hundred and fifteen Indians, with ten batteaux and seventy canoes.

The American garrison at Fort Mackinac only numbered sixty-three persons, including five sick men and one drummer boy.

There were nine American vessels in the harbor, having on board forty-seven men. After the capitulation two other vessels arrived, with seven hundred packs of furs.

The British approach and attack were admirably managed. Success was out of the question from the low shore line on Haldiman bay at the foot of Fort Mackinac, so Captain Roberts landed at three in the morning of July 17th at a point on the northwest shore of the Island, known since that eventful day as "British Landing." The invaders cautiously marched the three or four miles across the Island and took up with their two field pieces a commanding position on the hill where Fort Holmes now stands, less than a quarter of a mile from sleeping Fort Mackinac. Their Indian allies dispersed themselves in the nearby woods, and all was so quietly done that no fort sentinel raised an alarm. Meantime Dousman had been landed by his captors on strict parole not to inform the fort, but to quietly summon all the village inhabitants to a place on the west side of the Island where a British detail would guard them against attack and massacre by the Indians.

Dr. Sylvester Day, U.S.A., was the surgeon of the Fort. Michael Dousman hurried to his house and told the inmates of the presence of the British on the island. Dr. Day immediately arose, and taking his family (one of whom, his son, later became General Hannibal Day, U.S.A.) went to the Fort and warned the garrison of the approach of the foe. Lieut. Hanks immediately placed his weak defense forces in preparation for attack as best he could.

On the British side were 306 white soldiers, and 715 savages, a total of 1,021. Holding Fort Mackinac was the pitiful American force of 57 all told. Above them at a short distance were their enemies, with cannon mounted and ready for action.

At eleven o'clock in the morning the British Captain Roberts sent, under a flag of truce, a demand for the immediate surrender of the fort. The messenger was accompanied by three American civilian Islanders, Messrs. Samuel Abbott, John Dousman and Ambrose Davenport, who had been taken prisoners. They urged upon Lieutenant Hanks, as did his own officers, the futility of armed resistance, pointing out that defeat was certain at the hands of an overwhelming force, and that any delay in surrender would result without question in an Indian massacre not only of the garrison but of the women and children of both the fort and the village. Hanks wisely yielded to circumstances he could not control and promptly surrendered the fort.

From the archives of the United States War department we may read the official report made on August 4th, 1812, by Lieutenant Hanks to General Hull at Detroit, commanding the Northwest U. S. army at Detroit headquarters, stating the facts of the surrender of Fort Mackinac, and asking the appointment of a military court of inquiry to pass on his handling of the situation:

<hr>

Detroit, August 4th, 1812

Sir: I take the earliest opportunity to acquaint Your Excellency of the surrender of the garrison of Michilimackinac, under my command, to his Britannic Majesty's forces under the command of Captain Charles Roberts, on the 17th ultimo, the particulars of which are as follows: On the 16th, I was informed by the Indian Interpreter that he had discovered from an Indian that the several nations of

Indians then at St. Joseph (a British garrison, distant about forty miles) intended to make an immediate attack on Michilimackinac.

I was inclined, from the coolness I had discovered in some of the principal chiefs of the Ottawa and Chippewa nations, who had but a few days before professed the greatest friendship for the United States, to place confidence in this report.

I immediately called a meeting of the American gentlemen at that time on the island, in which it was thought proper to dispatch a confidential person to St. Joseph to watch the motions of the Indians.

Michael Dousman, captain of the militia, was thought the most suitable for this service. He embarked about sunset, and met the British forces within ten or fifteen miles of the island, by whom he was made prisoner and put on his parole of honor. He was landed on the island at daybreak, with positive directions to give me no intelligence whatever. He was also instructed to take the inhabitants of the village, indiscriminately, to a place on the west side of the island where their persons and property should be protected by a British guard, but should they go to the Fort, they would be subject to a general massacre by the savages, which would be inevitable if the garrison fired a gun. This information I received from Doctor Day, who was passing through the village when every person was flying for refuge to the enemy. I immediately, on being informed of the approach of the enemy, placed ammunition, etc., in the block houses; ordered every gun charged, and made every preparation for action. About 9 o'clock I could discover that the enemy were in possession of the heights that commanded the Fort, and one piece of their artillery directed to the most defenseless part of the garrison. The Indians at this time were to be seen in great numbers in the edge of the woods.

At half-past 11 o'clock the enemy sent in a flag of truce, demanding a surrender of the Fort and Island to his Britannic Majesty's forces. This, Sir, was the first information I had of the declaration of war; I, however, had anticipated it, and was as well prepared to meet such an event as I possibly could have been with the force under my command, amounting to 57 effective men, including officers. Three American gentlemen, who were prisoners, were permitted to accompany the flag; from them I ascertained the strength of the enemy to be from nine hundred to one thousand strong, consisting of regular troops, Canadians and savages; that they had two pieces of artillery, and were provided with ladders and ropes for the purpose of scaling the works, if necessary.

After I had obtained this information, I consulted my officers, and also the American gentlemen present, who were very intelligent men; the result of which was, that it was impossible for the garrison to hold out against such a superior force. In this opinion I fully concurred, from the conviction that it was the only measure that could prevent a general massacre. The Fort and garrison were accordingly surrendered.

The enclosed papers exhibit copies of the correspondence between the officer commanding the British forces and myself, and of the articles of capitulation. This subject involved questions of a peculiar nature; and I hope, Sir, that my demands and protests will meet the approbation of my government. I cannot allow this opportunity to escape without expressing my obligation to Doctor Sylvester Day, for the service he rendered me in conducting this correspondence.

In consequence of this unfortunate affair, I beg leave, Sir, to demand that a Court of Inquiry may be ordered to investigate all the facts connected with it; and I do further request, that the court may

be especially directed to express their opinion on
the merits of the case.

> I have the honour to be, Sir, etc.,
> Porter Hanks,
> Lieutenant of Artillery.

To His Excellency General Hull,
  Commanding the N. W. Army.

P. S. The following particulars relating to the
British force were obtained after the capitulation,
from a source that admits of no doubt:

Regular troops (including 4 officers.) 46
Canadian Militia 260
                                                        ———
    Total 306
Savages:
Sioux 56
 Winnebagoes 48
Menomonees 39
Chippewas and Ottawas 572
                                                        ———
    Total 1021

It may also be remarked that one hundred and
fifty Chippewas and Ottawas joined the British two
days after the capitulation. P. H.

TERMS OF THE SURRENDER

MICHILIMACKINAC, Mich., July 17th, 1812.

CAPITULATION

Agreed upon between Captain Charles Roberts,
commanding his Britannic Majesty's forces, on the
one part, and Lieutenant Porter Hanks, commanding the forces of the United States, on the other:

ARTICLES

I. The Fort of Michilimackinac shall immediately be surrendered to the British forces.   Granted.

MAJOR ANDREW HUNTER HOLMES
Gallant officer who was killed in the Battle of Mackinac Island

II. The garrison shall march out with the honours of war, lay down their arms, and become prisoners of war, and shall be sent to the United States of America by his Britannic Majesty. Not to serve in this war until regularly exchanged; and for the due performance of this article the officers pledge their word of honour.   Granted.

III. All the merchant vessels in the harbour, with their cargoes, shall be in the possession of their respective owners.   Granted.

IV. Private property shall be held sacred. Granted.

V. All citizens of the United States of America who shall not take the oath of allegiance to his Britannic Majesty, shall depart with their property from the island in one month from the date hereof. Granted.

(Signed) CHARLES ROBERTS,
              Commanding H. B. Majesty's forces.
          PORTER HANKS,
              Commanding the forces of the United
              States.

The British took immediate possession, their officers being hard put to restrain the savage allies from their peculiar atrocities. The British flag again waved over old Fort Mackinac, and the United States garrison laid down its arms, "with the honors of war", and became prisoners. It was promised that the officers and men would be returned to the United States under their pledge not to again serve in this war, unless regularly exchanged for British prisoners.

CHAPTER FOUR

Thus took place on historic Mackinac the first action in the war of 1812, just as it had been the scene of the last British surrender of territory following the war of the Revolution. Shortly afterwards General Hull surrendered the American post at Detroit and used as his excuse for its weak defense the claim that "the surrender of Michilimackinac opened the northern hive of hostile Indians, and they were swarming down on Detroit from every direction". One historian of that day wrote: "Hull was conquered at Mackinac".

The American prisoners were sent from Mackinac Island to Detroit, arriving there August 4th, thence to Fort Fayette, where Pittsburg, Pa., now stands, where a roll shows them to have been mustered on the 17th of November, 1812.

Lieutenant Hanks was killed August 16, while still on parole, by a shot fired from the Canadian side, while he was standing in the gateway of the fort at Detroit.

The capture of Mackinac gave the British not only new prestige in the Northwest but delivered into their hands valuable stores, furs and supplies, as well as considerable shipping then in the harbor. Also it gave them the key to the fur trade and the entire command of the upper lakes. Captain Roberts lost no time in seeking to prevent for his occupation the same strategy which had won Mackinac

for the King.   He proceeded immediately to
strengthen his position by building a strong earth-
work on the high hill north of the fort, re-inforced it
with heavy timbers and named it "Fort George" in
honor of his sovereign.   Impressed to involuntary
labor in this fortress construction were many able
bodied Island civilians, each man being forced to
give three days work with pick and shovel under
the stern eye of a British officer.

Captain Roberts, a semi-invalid, was relieved
in command by Captain Bullock in 1813, who early
in 1814 stepped aside for Lieut. Colonel Robert
McDouall, a vigorous and seasoned officer.   Learning that the Americans had mustered considerable strength and were building a fort at Prairie du
Chien on the Mississippi, Col. McDouall raised a
volunteer force which proceded down the lakes immediately and captured the embryo American post.

The year before, 1813, Detroit had been re-
taken by the Americans, and it was determined to
also re-capture Mackinac Island.   A combined naval and military expedition for this purpose left
Detroit on July 3rd, 1814, including seven war vessels under Commodore Sinclair and a land force of
750 men led by Lieut. Colonel George Grogan.
Their objectives also included the destruction by fire
of the English post at St. Joseph Island and the taking of a large supply base at Sault Ste. Marie.
After this latter successful sally, in charge of Major
Andrew Hunter Holmes, the American expedition
turned to its main errand, the re-capture of Mackinac Island and its important fort.

The combined American naval and land forces arrived off Mackinac Island on July 26th, 1814. They quickly discovered that the British had built fortifications on the hill above Fort Mackinac, the self-same point of attack advantage which had compelled the surrender of the Americans in 1821. Commodore Sinclair studied the Island from the deck of his sloop of war, "Niagara", and found approach or landing either impossible or unsafe at nearly every point along the shore. He later reported that he could not fire on Fort Mackinac because its elevation was so high that it was impossible to raise his cannon sufficiently to reach the fort walls.

For eight days the flotilla cruised about the vicinity, not close enough for action on either side. Col. Grogan realized that he could not carry Fort Mackinac by storm and finally decided to land his forces and "annoy the enemy by gradual and slow approaches". He believed he might establish and fortify a temporary stronghold, from which his attack could well be based. It was his hope and belief that in such case the Indian and Canadian allies of the British would leave the Island.

Learning from an informant familiar with the Island geography that a landing might be effected on the low beach line at the west side of Mackinac Island he dis-embarked his command, under the protection of the guns of the naval vessels of Sinclair, near the point where the British had done the same thing two years before, then and now known as British Landing.

Colonel McDouall, the British commander at Fort Mackinac, had for a week or more watched every move made by the threatening American forces, and his spies doubtless told of the preparations to make, and the actual making of, a west coast landing. He quickly gathered his own soldiers and his Indians in an ambush some distance inland, and waited for the assured attack. Meantime the Americans had proceeded up the slight incline leading from British Landing to the open fields a half mile or so towards the center of the Island, opposite the present Wa-Wash-Ka-Mo golf course. Suddenly from behind trees and bushes a disastrous fire was opened upon them by the Indians. At the same time they confronted rough breastworks behind which British cannon blazed away.

Col. Grogan endeavored to quickly change his position and extend his lines to gain the enemy's rear. This flank movement had scarcely begun, however, when from an Indian ambush a sudden volley brought down Major Holmes and Captain Desha, the next officer in rank. Immediate confusion resulted in the American lines, which was only partly checked by a charge and the bringing up of a piece of light artillery. It was at once apparent that the attack was hopeless, what with the loss of Major Holmes, the wounding of Captain Robert Desha, and the mortal wounds which had brought down Captain Isaac Van Horne, Jr., and Lieutenant Hezekiah Jackson, together with several non-commissioned officers and twelve privates.

Retreat to the ships was hastily ordered and the next morning, under a flag of truce, the body of

Major Holmes was recovered from the British and taken aboard the "Niagara". Thus ended in defeat for the Stars and Stripes the costly battle of Mackinac Island. On August 6th Col. Grogan discharged his militia, and returned two regular companies to Detroit. His final report says: "With my remaining three companies I shall attempt to destroy the enemy's establishment at the head of the Naw-taw-wa-sa-ga River."

Turning again to the Washington archives of the Army and Navy we find the official reports of both Colonel Grogan and Commodore Sinclair anent the disastrous attempt to recapture Fort Mackinac from the British. These reports are given here verbatim:

*   *   *

BATTLE OF MICHILIMACKINAC
Report of Col. George Grogan.
Aboard U. S. S. Niagara, Off Thunder Bay,
August 9th, 1814.

Sir: We left Fort Gratiot (head of the straits St. Clair) on the 12th ult. and imagined that we should arrive in a few days at Malshadash Bay. At the end of a week, however, the commodore from the want of pilots acquainted with that unfrequented part of the lake, despaired of being able to find a passage through the islands into the bay, and made for St. Joseph's, where he anchored on 20th day of July. After setting fire to the fort of St. Joseph's, which seemed not to have been recently occupied, a detachment of infantry and artillery, under Major Holmes, was ordered to Sault St. Mary's, for the purpose of breaking up the enemy's establishment at that place. For particulars relative to the successful execution of this order, I beg leave to refer you to Major Holmes' report herewith enclosed.

Finding on my arrival at Michilimackinac, on the 26th ult, that the enemy had strongly fortified the height overlooking the old Fort of Mackinac, I at once despaired of being able with my small force, to carry the place by storm, and determined (as the only course remaining) on landing and establishing myself on some favorable position, whence I could be enabled to annoy the enemy by gradual and slow approaches, under cover of my artillery, in which I should have the superiority in point of metal.   I was urged to adopt this step by another reason, not a little cogent; could a position be taken and fortified on the island, I was well aware that it would either induce the enemy to attack me in my strongholds, or force his Indians and Canadians (the most efficient, and only disposable force) off the island, as they would be very unwilling to remain in my neighborhood after a permanent footing had been taken.   On inquiry, I learned from individuals who had lived many years on the island, that a position desirable as I might wish, could be found at the west end, and therefore immediately made arrangements for disembarking. A landing was effected on the 4th inst., under cover of the guns of the shipping, and being quickly formed, had advanced to the edge of the field spoken of for a camp, when intelligence was conveyed to me, that the enemy was ahead, and a few seconds more brought us a fire from his battery of four pieces, firing shot and shells.

After reconnoitering his position, which was well selected, (his line reached along the edge of the woods, at the further extremity of the field and covered by a temporary breast work) I determined on changing my position (which was now two lines, the militia forming the front) by advancing Major Holmes' battalion of regulars on the right of the

OFFICERS' STONE QUARTERS, FORT MACKINAC

Showing picture of Dr. William Beaumont and monument erected in his honor.

militia, thus to outflank him, and by a vigorous effort to gain his rear.   The movement was immediately ordered, but before it could be executed, a fire
was opened by some Indians posted in a thick wood
near our right, which proved fatal to Major Holmes
and severely wounded Captain Desha the next officer in rank.   This unlucky fire, by depriving us of
the services of our most valuable officers, threw
that part of the line into confusion from which the
best exertions of the officers were not able to recover it.   Finding it impossible to gain the enemy's
left, owing to the impenetrable thickness of the
woods, a charge was ordered to be made by the
regulars immediately against the front.   This
charge, although made in some confusion, served to
drive the enemy back into the woods, from whence
an annoying fire was kept up by the Indians.

Lieut. Morgan was ordered up with a light
piece to assist the left, now particularly galled; the
excellent practice of this brought the enemy to fire
at a longer distance.   Discovering that this disposition from whence the enemy had just been driven
(and which had been represented to me as so high
and commanding) was by no means tenable, from
being interspersed with thickets, and intersected in
every way by ravines, I determined no longer to ex-
pose my force to the fire of an enemy deriving
every advantage which could be obtained from
numbers and a knowledge of the position, and
therefore ordered an immediate retreat towards
the shipping.   This affair, which cost us many valuable lives, leaves us to lament the fall of that gallant
officer, Major Holmes, whose character is so well
known to the war department.   Captain Van
Horne of the 19th Infantry and Lieut. Jackson of
the 24th Infantry, both brave intrepid young men,
fell wounded at the head of their respective com-
mands.

The conduct of all my officers on this occasion merits my approbation. Captain Desha, of the 24th Infantry, although wounded, continued with his command until forced to retire from faintness through loss of blood. Captains Saunders, Hawkins and Sturges, with every subaltern of that battalion, acted in the most exemplary manner. Ensign Bryan, 2nd Rifle Regiment, acting adjutant to the battalion, actively forwarded the wishes of the commanding officer. Lieuts. Hickman, 28th Infantry, and Hyde of the U. S. Marines, who commanded the reserve, claim my particular thanks for their activity in keeping that command in readiness to meet any exigency. I have before mentioned Lieut. Morgan's activity; his two assistants, Lieut. Pickett and Mr. Peters, conductor of artillery, also merit the name of good officers.

The militia were wanting in no part of their duty. Colonel Cotgreave, his officers and soldiers, deserve the warmest approbation; my acting assistant adjutant general, Captain N. H. Moore, 28th Infantry, with volunteer Adjutant McComb, were prompt in delivering my orders.

Captain Gratiot of the engineers, who volunteered his services as adjutant on the occasion, gave me valuable assistance. On the morning of the 5th, I sent a flag to the enemy, to enquire into the state of the wounded (two in number), who were left on the field, and to request permission to bring away the body of Major Holmes, which was also left, owing to the unpardonable neglect of the soldiers in whose hands he was placed. I am happy in assuring you that the body of Major Holmes is secured, and will be buried at Detroit with becoming honors. I shall discharge the militia tomorrow, and will send them down, together with two regular companies to Detroit.

With the remaining three companies I shall attempt to destroy the enemy's establishment in the head of Naw-taw-wa-sa-ga River, and if it be thought proper, erect a post at the mouth of this river.

Very respectfully, I have the honor to remain, sir, your obedient servant.

G. GROGAN,

Lieut. Col. 2nd Riflemen

To Hon. J. Armstrong,
   Secretary of War.

———

REPORT OF KILLED, WOUNDED AND MISSING.

August 4th, 1814.

On Board the U. S. Sloop of War Niagara, 11th August, 1814.

Artillery—Wounded, three privates.

Infantry—17th Regiment; Killed, five privates; wounded, two sergeants, two corporals, fifteen privates. Two privates since dead. Two privates missing.

19th Regiment—Wounded, one captain, nineteen privates. Captain Isaac Van Horne, Jr., since dead—one private since dead.

24th Regiment—Killed, five privates; wounded, one captain, one lieutenant, three sergeants, one musician, five privates. Captain Robert Desha severely; Lieut. Hezekiah Jackson since dead—one sergeant since dead.

Grand total—One major and twelve privates killed; two captains, one lieutenant, six sergeants, three corporals, one musician and thirty-eight privates wounded. Two privates missing.

The above return exhibits a true statement of the killed, wounded and missing in the affair of the 4th instant.

H. H. MOORE,
Captain 28th Infantry.
Acting Assistant Adjutant General.

REPORT OF CAPTAIN SINCLAIR

United States Sloop of War Niagara Off Thunder Bay, August 9th, 1814.

Sir: I arrived off Michilimackinac on the 26th July; but owing to a tedious spell of bad weather, which prevented our reconnoitering, or being able to procure a prisoner who could give us information of the enemy's Indian force, which, from several little skirmishes we had on an adjacent island (Round Island), appeared to be very great, we did not attempt a landing until the 4th inst., and it was then made more with a view to ascertain positively the enemy's strength, than with any possible hope of success; knowing, at the same time, that I could effectually cover their landing and retreat to the ships, from the position I had taken within 300 yards of the beach.

Col. Grogan would never had landed, even with this protection, being positive, as he was, that the Indian force alone on the island, with the advantages they had, were superior to him, could he have justified himself to his government, without having stronger proof than appearances, that he could not effect the object in view. Mackinac is, by nature, a perfect Gibraltar, being a high inaccessible rock on every side, except the west, from which to the heights, you have near two miles to pass through a wood, so thick that our men were shot in every direction, and within a few yards of them, without being able to see the Indians who did it; and a height was scarcely gained before there was another within 50 or 100 yards commanding it, where breastworks were erected and cannon opened on them. Several of those were charged and the enemy driven from them; but it was soon found the further our troops advanced the stronger the enemy became, and the weaker and more bewildered our forces were; several of the commanding officers were picked out and killed or wounded by the savages, without seeing any of them. The men were getting lost and falling into confusion, natural under such circumstances, which demanded an immediate retreat, or a total defeat and general massacre must have ensued. This was conducted in a masterly manner by Col. Grogan, who had lost the aid of that valuable and ever to be lamented officer, Major Holmes, who, with Captain VanHorn, was killed by the Indians.

The enemy were driven from many of their strongholds; but such was the impenetrable thickness of the woods, that no advantage gained could be profited by. Our attack would have been made immediately under the lower fort, that the enemy might not have been able to use his Indian force to such advantage as in the woods, having discovered by drawing a fire from him in several instances, that I had greatly the superiority of metal of him; but its site being over 120 feet above the water, I could not, when near enough to do him an injury, elevate sufficiently to batter it. Above this, nearly as high again, he has another strong fort, commanding every point on the island, and almost perpendicular on all sides. Col. Grogan not deeming it prudent to make a second attempt upon this place, and having ascertained to a certainty that the only naval force the enemy have upon the lakes consists of one schooner of four guns, I have determined to despatch the "Lawrence" and "Caledonia" to Lake Erie immediately, believing their services in transporting our armies there will be wanting; and it being important that the sick and wounded, amounting to about 100, and that part of the detachment not necessary to further our future operations, here, should reach Detroit without delay. By an intelligent prisoner, captured in the "Mink," I ascertained this, and that the mechanics and others sent across from York during the winter were for the purpose of building a flotilla to transport re-inforcements and supplies to Mackinac. An attempt was made to transport them by the way of Matchadash, but it was found impracticable, from all the portages being a morass; that they then resorted to a small river called Nautawasaga, situated to the south of Matchadash, from which there is a portage of three leagues over a good road to Lake Simcoe. This place was never known until pointed out to them last summer by an Indian. This river is very narrow, and has six or eight feet water in it about three miles up, and is then a muddy, rapid shallow for 45 miles up to the portage, where their armada was built, and their storehouses are now situated. The navigation is dangerous and difficult, and so obscured by rocks and bushes that no stranger could ever find it. I have, however, availed myself of the means of discovering it.

I shall also blockade the mouth of French River until the fall; and those being the only two channels of communication by which Mackinac can possibly be supplied, and their provisions at this time being extremely short, I think they will be starved into a surrender.

This will also cut off all fort supplies, and will also cut off supplies to the Northwest Company, who are now nearly starving, and their furs on hand can only find transportation by the way of Hudson Bay. At this place I calculate on falling in with their schooner, which, it is said, has gone there for a load of provisions, and a message sent to her not to venture out while we are on the lake.

Very respectfully, I have the honor to remain, Sir,

Your obedient servant,
ARTHUR SINCLAIR

To Hon. Wm. Jones,
    Secretary of the Navy.

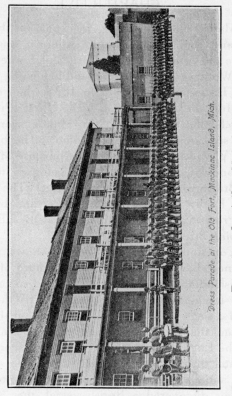

Dress Parade at the Old Fort, Mackinac Island, Mich.

Dress parade at the old fort, 1852.

CHAPTER FIVE

Major Holmes' body was put on board a schooner and sent to Detroit, where it was buried in the old cemetery on the corner of Larned Street and Woodward Avenue, on land belonging to "The First Protestant Society." In 1834 when excavating for the building of "The First Protestant Church" the remains of Major Holmes were found with six cannon balls in the coffin. The balls had been placed in the coffin for the purpose of sinking the body if danger chanced of being captured by the British while on its way to Detroit. The remains were finally placed in a new casket and buried in the Protestant cemetery near Gratiot, Beaubien and Antoine Streets, Detroit.

Commodore Sinclair's report shows that he had not abandoned the ultimate capture of Mackinac Island and its fort. Having failed so completely by force of arms, he determined to try the strategy of a siege. His plan was to starve out the garrison and thus force its surrender. Supplies and food for the English on Mackinac could only come from Canada through the Georgian Bay route.

Cautiously cruising in that vicinity Commodore Sinclair discovered a British vessel, the "Nancy", hove to under the protection of a block house near the mouth of the Notawasaga river, and loaded to the gunwales with six months supply of provisions for the Mackinac Island fort. The Americans made a surprise attack, blew up the block house and destroyed the "Nancy" and her cargo. The American sloops, "Tigress" and "Scorpion" were detailed to continue the blockade of the British garrison at Mackinac, already severely suffering from the scarcity of provisions. So low had run the Island fort supply of food that a loaf of bread was selling for one dollar and the soldiers were killing their horses for meat.

Regarding this distress, resulting from the American marine blockade, an English officer wrote of this time: "The enemy established a blockade by which they intercepted our supplies. We had but a small store of provisions and the commander grew very anxious. The garrison was put on short rations, horses were killed and salted down. At length we saw ourselves on the verge of starvation with no relief from any quarter".

Added to the troubles of the British garrison were marked shrinkings in the at best half hearted friendship of the Island Indians. They were evidently holding their loyalty and aid to see whether the British or the Americans would eventually triumph.

Word came to Col. McDouall of the destruction of the blockhouse and the "Nancy's" stores of provisions, brought to the Island by Lieut. Worsley and seventeen sailors of His Majesty's navy, who escaped during the American attack. Forced to desperation the doughty colonel mustered a volunteer contingent of seventy from the Island, including sailors, soldiers and Indians, under the command of Lieut. Worsley.

Against what appeared to be hopeless odds this gallant British company set out in small boats for the eastern Canadian waters seeking the "Tigress" and the "Scorpion", the former being soon discovered at anchor off St. Joseph's Island. Coming alongside in the darkness the British clambered aboard and after a short and sharp hand to hand engagement captured the vessel and its surprised crew. The prisoners were the next day sent to Mackinac.

As a decoy the American flag was retained over the "Tigress" and when, a day or two later, its sister ship "Scorpion" came to port, unaware of the capture, a second brief engagement resulted in hauling down the stars and stripes and raising in their place the flag of Great Britain.

The arrival at Mackinac Island of the captured American vessels, containing supplies of both food and ammunition, brought joy to the garrison and the village, for food had become so scarce during the American blockade that "starvation might have caused a surrender in less than a fortnight".

The treaty of Ghent ended the second and last war between the United States and Great Britain in 1815, the year after the battle of Mackinac Island. By the terms of the treaty Mackinac Island was forever lost to the British. It was a hard blow to the ambitious and able Col. McDouall who wrote Lieut. Bulger, his second in command: "Our negotiators as usual have been duped. As usual they have shown themselves profoundly ignorant of the concerns of this part of the Empire. I am penetrated with grief at the loss of this fine Island—a fortress built by nature."

The raising of the American flag for all time over Fort Mackinac was also a severe blow to the British fur traders, in which dilemma they had the sympathy of the militant English colonel and of the Governor of Canada. The King's men were removed to Drummond Island, forty or fifty miles to the east and over the Canadian line, where a fort was built near a good harbor. Colonel McDouall planned a post stronger than the one he had been compelled to evacuate at Mackinac. But his plans did not develop, nor did the Indian fur trade follow the British flag. Then, in 1822, after much disputation, Drummond Island was declared to be American soil, and the British were forced to again move, this time to their old location on St. Joseph's Island. Soon this latter post was abandoned.

In this manner the flag of Great Britain left forever the Mackinac country.

CHAPTER SIX

It is outside the province of this book to dwell upon the importance and growth of the American fur trade which centered on Mackinac Island, and grew apace after the restoration of the Island to the United States. Here John Jacob Astor, Robert Stuart and Ramsay Crooks organized and carried on the business of the American Fur Company, first corporation in the United States.

However, it is a privilege to pause for a few moments and read the account written by that eminent citizen of Mackinac Island and later a distinguished civic leader in old Chicago, Gurdon S. Hubbard, employe of the American Fur Company, of his arrival at Mackinac and his word picture of its unique setting nearly one hundred years ago. His story follows:

"We arrived at Mackinac Island on July 4th, 1818. Here lived old voyagers, worn out with the hard service incident to their calling, with their families of half-breeds. Only a few of the inhabitants engaged in trade. Mrs. Mitchell, an energetic, enterprising woman, the wife of Dr. Mitchell, a surgeon of the English army, and stationed at Drummond's Island, had a store and small farm. Michael Dousman, Edward Biddle, and John Drew were also merchants, all depending on trading with the Indians.

"These merchants, to a very great extent, were under the influence of the American Fur Company, purchasing most of their goods from them, and selling to them their furs and peltries. This island was the headquarters of the American Fur Company, and here I first learned something of the working and discipline of that mammoth corporation, and took my first lessons in the life of an Indian trader, a life which I followed exclusively for ten consecutive years. Here, also, was located Fort Mackinac, at that time garrisoned by one or two companies of United States troops. The village had a population of about five hundred, mostly of Canadian French and of mixed Indian blood, whose chief occupation was fishing in summer and hunting in winter. There were not more than twelve white women on the island, the residue of the female population being either all or part Indian.

"Here, during the summer months, congregated the traders employed by the Fur Company, bringing their collections from their several trading posts, which extended from the British dominions on the north and the Missouri River in the west, south, and east to the white settlements; in fact, to all the Indian hunting grounds, so that when all were collected they added three thousand or more to the population.

"The Indians from the shores of the upper lakes, who made this island a place of resort, numbered from two to three thousand or more. Their wigwams lined the entire beach two or three rows deep, and, with the tents of the traders, made the island a scene of life and animation.

"The voyageurs were fond of fun and frolic, and the Indians indulged in their love of liquor, and, by the exhibition of their war, medicine, and other dances and sports, often made both night and day hideous with their yells. These voyageurs were all Canadian French, and were the only people fitted for the life they were compelled to endure, their cheerful temperament and happy disposition making them contented under the privations and hardships incident to their calling.

"At the time of our arrival, all the traders from the North and the Great West had reached the island with their returns of furs collected from the Indians during the previous winter, which were being counted and appraised, and the profit or loss of each "outfit" ascertained.

"The work of assorting required expert judges of furs, a nice discrimination between the different grades being necessary, as prices varied very greatly, there being as many as six grades. Marten (sable), for example, being classed as extra fine dark, number one dark, number two dark, number one fine brown, number two fine brown, number one fine, common, number two common, number three common, good, out of season, inferior, damaged, and worthless. The value of the fur of this animal depended as much on color as fineness, and was found in the greatest variety of shades of color, and, with the exception of silver gray fox, was the most valuable. Mink, muskrat, raccoon, lynx, wild cat, fox, wolverine, badger, otter, beaver, and other small fur animals, received the same care, except there were fewer grades of quality. In bear skins,

The John Jacob Astor House, Mackinac Island, 1833.

only, were there more than four grades, but in those the discrimination was nearly equal to marten, being extra fine black 'she", number two ditto, fine number one, number two ditto, and fine, coarse, and numbers one, two and three "he" bear. Deer skins required but little skill in assorting; they were classed as red doe, red buck, blue doe, blue buck, season doe, season buck, out of season, and damaged.

"The commanders of outfits were deeply interested in the assortment of their furs, and were very watchful to see that justice was done them; for upon this depended their balance sheets of profit or loss. Hence, frequent disputes arose as to the grade and value of the skins.

"It was my business to make a second count in order to verify the first. The first count was entered on a book not seen by me, and if mine corresponded with it, the furs were placed in a frame, pressed, marked, and rolled into the shipping wareroom. If, however, my count did not agree with the first, I was required to make a second count, and if there was still a discrepancy, a third person was called upon to recount them. This work took about two months, the working hours being from five o'clock in the morning to twelve noon, and from one to seven in the afternoon, and, as I was obliged to maintain a stooping posture, was severely fatiguing.

"About one hundred voyageurs were detailed to assist in this business, and were kept under strict discipline. Most of them were experienced, and were generally contented and happy, each working with a will, knowing that Mackinac fatigue duty came but once in four years, and that if they lived through the succeeding three years, their time at headquarters could be spent in comparative ease and comfort.

"The daily ration issued by the commissary to a mess of from six to ten men, consisted of one pint of lyed or hulled and dried corn, with from two to four ounces of tallow, to each man; and this was all that they received, except that on Saturday flour was given them for Sunday pancakes. It would seem that this was a very short and light ration for healthy, hard-working men, but it was quite sufficient, and generally more than they could consume. It was invariably liked by them, and it was found that they could endure more hardships on this than on a diet of bread and meat.

"The force of the Company, when all were assembled on the island, comprised about four hundred clerks and traders, together with some two thousand voyageurs. About five hundred of these were quartered in barracks, one hundred lived in the agency house, and the others were camped in tents and accommodated in rooms of the Islanders.

"Dances and parties were given every night by the residents of the island in honor of the traders, and they, in their turn, reciprocated with balls and jollifications, which, though not as elegant and costly as those of the present day, were sufficiently so to drain from the participants all the hard earnings of the winter previous.

"In each "brigade," or outfit, was to be found one who, from superior strength or bravery, was looked upon as the "bully" of that crew of voyageurs, and who, as a distinguished mark, wore a black feather in his cap. These "bullies" were generally good fighters, and were always governed by the rules of fair play. It was a rule, and was expected, that they should fight each other; hence it was not an uncommon thing to see a fight. The vanquished one gave up his black feather to the conqueror, or shook hands with him, and they both joined with the lookers on in a glass of beer or whisky as good-naturedly as though nothing unpleasant had occurred.

"The majority of the inhabitants of the island were of mixed blood—Canadian and Indian—and those who were of pure blood, and were heads of families, had Indian wives. Their children, though uneducated, were usually bright and intelligent, and fond of finery, dancing, and other amusements. There were a few of the half-breeds who had received a common education, either in English or French, which was generally of little use to them, as they were mostly too lazy or proud to earn a livelihood.

"Among the Indian or part Indian women who were, or had been, married to white husbands, were found some of great intellectual capacity, who carried on an extensive trade with the Indians, one of whom was the Mrs. Mitchell before referred to. She had a store and a farm, both under excellent management, and her children had been well educated in Canada. This woman's husband was a

Scotchman and a surgeon in the English army, and while the Island of Mackinac was in the possession of England he was stationed there. Removing afterwards to Drummond's Island, he rarely visited his family, though only fifty miles distant. He was a man of strong prejudices, hated the "Yankees," and would hold no social intercourse with them.

"Mrs. Mitchell was quite the reverse, and being rather partial to the "Yankees," treated them with great consideration; she was a fine housekeeper and owned one of the best houses on the island; she was fond of good society, very hospitable, and entertained handsomely, conversing in French and English, both of which she spoke fluently.

"Another of these women was Mrs. LaFromboise, who also traded with the Indians in the interior, usually up the Grand River of Michigan; her daughter was highly educated, and married the commanding officer at Fort Mackinaw, Capt. Benjamin K. Pierce, whose brother, Franklin, was later president of the United States.

"Mrs. LaFromboise could read and write, and was a perfect lady in her manners and conversation; she was a widow, her husband, who was a trader, having been shot and killed by an Indian on the Mississippi River; she took his place and business and accumulated considerable money. She was afterwards employed on a salary by the American Fur Company.

"It was the policy of the American Fur Company to monopolize the entire fur trade of the Northwest; and to this end they engaged fully nineteen-twentieths of all the traders of that territory, and with their immense capital and influence succeeded in breaking up the business of any trader who refused to enter their service.

"Very soon after reaching Mackinac and making returns, the traders commenced organizing their crews and preparing their outfits for their return to winter quarters at their various trading posts, those destined for the extreme North being the first to receive attention. These outfits were called "brigades."

"The brigade destined for the Lake of the Woods, having the longest journey to make, was the first to depart. They were transported in boats called "batteaux," which very much resembled the boats now used by fishermen on the Great Lakes, except that they were larger, and were each manned by a crew of five men besides a clerk. Four of the men rowed while the fifth steered. Each boat carried about three tons of merchandise, together with the clothing of the men and rations of corn and tallow. No shelter was provided for the voyageurs, and their luggage was confined to twenty pounds in weight, carried in a bag provided for that purpose.

"The commander of the "brigade" took for his own use the best boat, and with him an extra man, who acted in the capacity of "orderly" to the expedition, and the will of the commander was the only law known. The clerks were furnished with salt pork, a bag of flour, tea and coffee, and a tent for shelter, and messed with the commander and orderly.

"A vast multitude assembled at the harbor to witness their departure, and when all was ready the boats glided from the shore, the crews singing some favorite boat song, while the multitude shouted their farewells and wishes for a successful trip and a safe return."

CHAPTER SEVEN

For more than forty years the military occupation of Fort Mackinac followed the peace time pursuits of the regular United States army. Far back in 1816 a detail from this fort had established itself at Fort Howard, on the west side of the Fox River at what is now Green Bay, Wisconsin.

In 1818 the Governor of Michigan Territory, the famous Lewis Cass, issued a proclamation setting forth as follows the boundaries of Michilimackinac county, and established its "seat of justice" at Mackinac Island:

* * *

A PROCLAMATION

"Whereas, the convenience of the citizens, and the due administration of justice, require that a new county should be established in the said territory;

"Now therefore, I do by these presents, and by the virtue of the Ordinance of Congress, July 13, 1787, lay out that part of the said territory, to which the Indian title has been extinguished, included within the following boundaries, namely: Commencing at the White Rock on the shore of Lake Huron, thence with the line of the county of Macomb, to the boundary line between the United States and the British Province of Upper Canada; thence with the said boundary line, to the western boundary of the said territory of Michigan; thence southerly, with the said western boundary, so far that a line drawn due west, from the dividing ground between the rivers which flow into Lake Superior, and those which flow south, will strike

Ancient Fort Holmes as accurately restored in 1936 on the hill overlooking Fort Mackinac.

the same; thence due east, to the said dividing ground, and with the same, to a point due north from Sturgeon Bay; thence south to the said bay; thence by the nearest line to the western boundary of the said territory, as the same was established by the act of Congress, passed, January 11, 1805, entitled "An Act to divide the Indian Territory into two separate governments'; thence with the same, to a point due west from the southwestern corner of the said county of Macomb; thence due east to the southwestern corner of the said County of Macomb; thence with the western boundary of the said county, to the place of the beginning, into a separate county, to be called the county of Michilimackinac.

"Given under my hand, at Detroit, the twenty-sixth day of October, in the year of our Lord one thousand eight hundred and eighteen, and of the Independence of the United States, the forty-third.
                                        "Lew. Cass."

                    *   *   *

In 1819 both village residents and Fort garrison were thrilled by the arrival in the harbor of the first steam propelled vessel on the Great Lakes, the S. S. "Walk-in-the-Water".

In 1820 Henry R. Schoolcraft, the eminent pioneer and Indian agent, after whom is named Schoolcraft county in Northern Michigan, arrived with Governor Lewis Cass on Mackinac Island, coming with a flotilla of canoes from Detroit. Their errand was to outline the boundaries of Michigan territory and the dramatic story of this hazardous and uncompleted enterprise may be read in the fine historical works of Schoolcraft available in the larger metropolitan and state libraries.

The annual report for 1828 on file in the Inspector General's department of the Army tells us that the Fort Mackinac garrison "will soon be reduced to a single company, for the one under command of Lieut. Charles F. Morton is under orders for Maine. This fort will in a short time be esteemed the most desirable of our infantry posts." A similar War department report in 1831 says: "This place (Mackinac Island) is healthy as usual—perhaps there is none more so in the United States."

Immediately after the American occupation of the Island the rustic building which the British had named Fort George was occupied for a short time by a detail from the main fort below. But it was soon abandoned and the building removed to the foot of the hill and used as a stable. Its brief military occupation under the American flag witnessed its being named Fort Holmes, in honor of the gallant officer who fell in the battle of Mackinac Island.

In 1936 the State Park commission and the Federal government, as a Works Progress Administration project, happily rebuilt the old fort on the original high ground, exactly on its original lines, so that today Fort Holmes, visible far out on the lakes, is a worthy monument to the brave soldier for whom it was named. It is of log construction with all the battlements and devices of pioneer fortress construction, and annually visited by thousands of Island travellers. Its complete restoration, from gleaming whitewashed stockade to inside powder magazine and commissary, compares with the similar restoration of old Fort Michilimackinac at Mackinaw City.

Fort Mackinac's garrison varied from the four companies of 1818 to the one company of 1828, and in the months between October 14th, 1839, and May 18, 1840, it held no troops except a skeleton guard. Again in October, 1856, the fort was evacuated by Major Thomas Williams' command, Co. 1, 4th U. S. Artillery, to be re-garrisoned the next May by Captain Arnold Jones and his detail of the 2nd U. S. Artillery.

On August 2nd, 1857, the Mackinac Island command, together with that from Fort Brady at Sault Ste. Marie, was ordered to the scene of the Indian hostilities at Fort Snelling, Minnesota.

Detailed at Fort Mackinac intermittently for more than forty years from 1854 to its final Federal evacuation in 1895 was an Island resident officer, whose record in service is a proud possession in Mackinac Island annals, Brevet Lieutenant Colonel John R. Bailey, U. S. Volunteers, Medical Corps, assistant surgeon and surgeon in active service during the Civil war and Special Medical Purveyor to the Army of the Tennessee in the field at Chattanooga. He was eminent both as soldier and physician, and his labors at Fort Mackinac covered four decades, taking out the years of his field service from 1861 to 1865. He was later a member of the Mackinac Island State Park commission, and he sleeps today on the historic island he loved so well. His history of "Mackinac, formerly Michilimackinac", was a best seller in the last years of the Nineteenth century, and the writer gratefully acknowledges the help of that history in the compilation of this book.

When the Civil war opened in 1861 the garrison of Fort Mackinac, under Capt. Henry C. Pratt, was ordered to the front, and the fort was left in charge of Ordnance Sergeant William Marshall until its re-occupation in May, 1862, by Michigan Volunteers, Company A of the Stanton Guards, commanded by Captain Grover S. Wormer, who had as prisoners of war three prominent Confederates, General William G. Harding, General Washington Barrows and Judge Joseph C. Guild. In September the garrison was moved to Detroit and the prisoners sent to Johnson's Island in Lake Erie to await exchange.

Since every United States soldier was needed at the front until the end of the war in 1865, Fort Mackinac had no garrison. A veteran reserve corps contingent remained for a few months service in the summer of 1866, and the regular army returned in 1867 (Company B, 43rd U. S. Infantry, Lieut. Col. John Mitchell Reed, first commanding) to remain until the ceding of the Fort and the entire military reservation conditionally to the State of Michigan by the Federal government in 1895.

Following the American re-possession of Mackinac Island, after the termination of the War of 1812 with England, the Federal government had released and sold a few private land claims to citizens of the village itself, but retained very much the largest share of Mackinac Island (estimated at close to eighty per cent) as a military reservation, including, of course, Old Fort Mackinac.

In 1873 United States Senator Thomas W. Ferry of Michigan, himself a native son of Mackinac

Island, brought about Congressional legislation by which all of the Island, excepting the fort itself (which remained as an occupied post by the United States army), was "dedicated and set apart as a national public park for health, comfort and pleasure". Thus was created on Mackinac Island the second of what has become the far flung series of United States National Parks. However, the Island was held in reserve for possible military purposes in times of peace, or "for complete occupation in time of war". It was under the exclusive jurisdiction of the Secretary of War, both as a National Park and as a possible military post.

Twenty two years later, in March, 1895, Michigan's Senator James McMillan put through the Congress an act authorizing "the Secretary of War, upon application of the Governor of Michigan, to turn over to the State of Michigan, for use as a state park, and for no other purpose, the military reservation and buildings, and the land of the National Park on Mackinac Island; provided, that whenever the state ceases to use the land for the purpose aforesaid, it shall revert to the United States."

The act making the State of Michigan conditional owner and administrator of Mackinac Island also provided for the appointment by the governor of a commission of five members to control the state park, serving without pay. For the 43 years since this Congressional action administration has been under the control of the Mackinac Island State Park commission, with the Governor as an ex-officio member. The park contains 1,041 acres, of which 500 are covered with hardwood and 400 acres with spruce, cedar, hemlock and other soft woods. It is said on authority that the Island park contains one or more of every kind of tree which is native to any part of Michigan. The park has forty miles of road, and sixty miles of Indian trails and paths. A boulevard shore drive embraces the outer coast, nearly nine miles long.

Michigan promptly accepted the famous Island park and fort, in trust, and orders were for the immediate evacuation of the U.S. regulars in garrison and the formal delivery of the property to the stewardship of the new State Park commission.

It was with sincere regret that the citizens of Mackinac Island watched the departure of the army late in 1895, as Lieut. Woodbridge Geary, 19th U. S. Infantry, led his men for the last time through the south sally port of the historic old fort.

The late Rev. Meade C. Williams, D.D., a well known student of history of the Straits section and long a trustee of the old Mission church on the Island, gave the following eloquent valedictory of the evacuation of Fort Mackinac in his book "Early Mackinac", now out of print, published years ago by Duffield & Company in New York:

"It is a matter of deep regret that the National Government should have forsaken the Island. For sentimental reasons, even had there been no other, the old fort should have been retained as a United States army post. A military seat which has two hundred years or more of history behind it is not often to be found in the western world. Indeed, with the possible exception of Ft. Marion, the old Spanish fortification at St. Augustine, Florida, it is doubtful if there be another on this continent which could boast of so long a period of continuous occupation as Old Fort Michilimackinac, which was established first at St. Ignace in the 17th century, then removed to Old Mackinaw (on the southern mainland) and since 1780 has been located on Mackinac Island."

It is a little known fact that the Michigan legislature of 1897 offered to return to the Federal government Fort Mackinac and its buildings, together with the ground designated as the "military reservation". Congress did not respond to this gesture promptly and it was later withdrawn and the act repealed by a subsequent state legislature.

Eagle Scout Honor Guard barracks on Fort Mackinac parade grounds.

CHAPTER EIGHT

Early in 1938 the National Park Service, an important branch of the U. S. Department of the Interior, having studied the dramatic history of Fort Mackinac, signified its willingness to designate it as an "Historical Monument", in common with Fort Marion in Florida and many other outstanding historical points throughout the country. It is possible that some future Michigan legislature will return the fort on Mackinac Island to the supervision and control of the National Park service, and its preservation and maintenance by the Federal government.

Old Fort Mackinac already owes a heavy debt to the U. S. National Park Service for the restoration work done in 1933 and 1934 under its supervision, with the help of a Civilian Conservation Camp. The impending danger of the great stone wall on the east side being undermined by flood waters was averted by permanent repairs, and rotting foundations of timber under many of the historic old buildings were replaced with solid stone and cement. The very exhaustive and analytical report of the National Park Service consulting architect, Warren L. Rindge, has already been referred to with sincere gratitude by those charged with the care and maintenance of Fort Mackinac.

The writer is happily permitted to quote from the able findings made after an extended study of Fort Mackinac by the Hon. Thomas M. Pitkin, assistant historian of the National Park Service, made available by Mr. Pitkin with the approval of the Hon. Arno B. Cammerer of Washington, D. C., director of the National Park Service of the Interior department under the Hon. Harold L. Ickes, Secretary of the Interior. Mr. Pitkin's report gives encouragement to all who are interested in the preservation of Northern Michigan's historic sites and offers food for thought to Michigan law makers. This eminent historian reported to Washington that:

"The importance of Fort Mackinac as an historic site derives not only from its significant associations in the exploration, exploitation and struggle for control in the Great Northwest, but also from the fact that it remains relatively unspoiled. At all other sites connected with the early history of the region the growth of cities or the vandal's hand have destroyed historic remains and changed the face of nature. Mackinac Island, however, still for the most part heavily wooded, shows the ancient contour which caused it to be called by the Indians "Michilimackinac, the Great Turtle". Here also the most ambitious military structures ever erected in the upper country still stand, a complex of stone and wooden defenses and buildings gleaming in whitewash and white paint.

"The Island, scene of most of the historic interest in the Straits area since 1780, has unusual historical remains of undisputed authenticity. It seems unquestioned that to date the history of the Old Northwest has not received its due share of the attention of the Federal government. It is interesting to recall in this connection that Mackinac Island

was the second National park ever created. The
fact that it was not adequately maintained and that
it was finally turned over to the State of Michigan
does not detract from the true national significance
of the Island."

Mr. Pitkin goes on to refer to the importance of
developing the museums on the old fort into "most
interesting educational exhibits", and suggests that
if, in the future, this historic site becomes a Federal
National Monument, the acquisition should include
Fort Michilimackinac park at Mackinaw City and,
if possible, the site of the ancient fortress of St.
Ignace, now being reconstructed in its original form.

For nearly twenty-five years the old stone Officers Quarters building on the fort has been used as an
Indian, military and colonial museum. In 1915 the
Hon. Edwin O. Wood, chairman of the State Park
Commission, presented to this museum an extensive
and valuable collection of ancient implements of
peace and war, most of them with a local coloring,
and to this splendid foundation there have been
added many exhibits of most interesting and instruc-
tive character.

In 1938 the old canteen building, adjoining the
stone quarters on the east, was also set apart for
museum purposes, and now contains many exhibits
of compelling interest, most of which are loaned to
the fort through the courtesy of the Historical Museum which is part of the Capitol building at Lan-
sing. All displays have been arranged and marked
by the competent curator appointed by the Park
commission, Miss Esther Fletcher of Kalamazoo.

Only once since the evacuation of the fort in 1895 have soldiers of the Regular U. S. army been on duty there. In 1934, through the courtesy of Major General Frank Parker, famous for long service at home and over-seas, who was in command of the Sixth Corps Army area, with headquarters in Chicago, a fractional company of the 2nd U. S. Infantry was detailed from Fort Brady, at Sault Ste. Marie, for a week's duty at Mackinac Island, and made their camp on the old parade ground. Once more the fort was "garrisoned", the stirring notes of the bugle heard throughout the day, and dress parades and salute to the colors part of the fixed routine. Attending also on that occasion was the fine band of the Menominee, Michigan, High School, under the direction of Octave C. Paquette. During the week a review was held with the personal attendance of General Parker and members of his staff, guests of the famous Grand Hotel on Mackinac. Visitor attendance broke all previous records during this temporary army "re-occupation", after an interval of 39 years.

Annually, "Army week" is fittingly celebrated on Mackinac Island, culminating in Beaumont Hospital day, when a group of patriotic women raise the funds necessary for the summer maintenance of the Beaumont Memorial Emergency hospital at the old fort.

At the foot of the Fort's main ramparts in Marquette park the Michigan Daughters of the American Revolution, some eight years ago, presented and erected a stone memorial tablet naming Mackinac as "the most historic spot in Michigan."

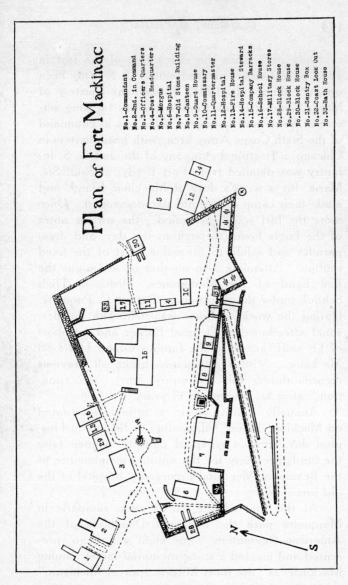

Plan of Fort Mackinac.

No.1–Commandant
No.2–2nd. in Command
No.3–Officer s Quarters
No.4–Post Headquarters
No.5–Morgue
No.6–Hospital
No.7–Old Stone Building
No.8–Canteen
No.9–Guard House
No.10–Commissary
No.11–Quartermaster
No.12–Hospital
No.13–Fire House
No.14–Hospital Steward
No.15–Company Barracks
No.16–School House
No.17–Military Stores
No.28–Block House
No.29–Block House
No.30–Block House
No.31–Sentry Box
No.32–Coast Look Out
No.33–Bath House

Plan of buildings on Fort Mackinac.

Across Nicolet Road, on the ground given by Michigan to the U. S. Coast Guard twenty or more years ago for a life saving station, stands one of the ancient cannon captured from the British on Lake Erie on Sept. 10, 1813, by the immortal Commodore Oliver H. Perry, whose report of the successful engagement is known to every school boy and girl in America: "We have met the enemy and they are ours."

Serving at Fort Mackinac between 1815 and 1895 were many officers, mostly young men, who later attained high rank in the army and distinguished themselves in active service in the Civil war and the War with Spain in 1898. Some of the earlier West Pointers who served here enlisted with the Confederate army in the southern states in which they were born. Among the Mackinac officers whose names were later heralded in broader fields of history may be included General Edwin V. Sumner (2nd Lieut., Fort Mackinac 1827); General Samuel T. Heintzelman (2nd Lieut. 1827); General Kirby Smith (2nd Lieut. 1829); General Silas Casey (captain 1845); and General Fred Steele (2nd Lieut. 1845) after whom a western Army post was later named. The Confederate General John C. Pemberton, who commanded Vicksburg against the Union Army forces under General Grant in 1863, was a Fort Mackinac lieutenant in 1840.

We stand in reverence at the entrance to the old Post Cemetery of Fort Mackinac, in a wooded glen a quarter of a mile north of the military reservation. Here sleep, "waiting the Judgment Day", more than 150 veterans of active and garrison duty in the United States army, enlisted in every war in which our country has engaged from the days of 1776 to 1917.

Some seventy of the graves hold "Unknown Soldiers" and the headstones simply read "A soldier of the United States". Every day of every year the flag they loved waves above their sepulchre. On each Memorial day, in charge of members of the American Legion, services are held at this sacred spot. Year after year, until failing health took him to an eastern Soldiers' Home, Sergeant Joseph Leggett, believed to be the oldest living veteran of actual army service on Fort Mackinac, undertook as a labor of love and patriotism the Memorial Day exercises at the Post Cemetery. The Athletic field on the military reservation on the Island was named in his honor in 1934 by the State Park Commission.

The crumbling head stones at the cemetery record the death in 1857 of Hospital Steward Judson J. Rogers, USA, who with his six year old son was drowned in the wreck of the steamer Champlain off Charlevoix, Michigan, on June 17th of that year; of Captain John Glitz, 2nd US Infantry, commanding Fort Mackinac, Nov. 6th, 1836; of Major Edwin E. Sellers, 10th US Inf., 1884; and Captain E. E. Gaskill, 1889.

Lieut. Colonel John R. Bailey was buried in the private family lot in the Protestant cemetery. Major Dwight H. Kelton, USA, who married Miss Annie Donnelly of the prominent Island family of that name, was buried with military rites at Arlington Cemetery, Washington, D. C.

In the center of the Post cemetery is mounted one of the cannon which formed the defenses of historic Fort Sumter at the beginning of the Civil war. On two sides of the pedestal upon which the cannon rests are tablets containing these words:

"On fame's eternal camping ground
    Their silent tents are spread;
While glory guards with solemn round
    The bivouac of the dead."

CHAPTER NINE

So this is the outlined story to date of Old Fort Mackinac on the Hill of History.

Every deeply worn stairway of these old barracks and quarters, every foot of this military reservation, every room in every ancient building, had they speech, might tell us dramatic incidents of peace and war, of love and hate, of tragedy and hardship, of sport and recreation, of pioneering and suffering, of barter and trade.

No words can tell the full story. All who love their country, and their flag will find a visit to Old Fort Mackinac, and indeed to all the historic Straits of Mackinac section, a pilgrimage worth while for young and old.

* * *

There is a grip at the heart strings as the flag we love is lowered at old Fort Mackinac in the evening with the call of the bugle and the presence of the color guard. It will again be raised at sunrise, as it has been for more than a century, every day of every year, and will be, God willing, down the years to the end of time.

> Our Father's God, to Thee,
> Author of Liberty,
> To Thee we sing.
> Long may our land be bright
> With freedom's holy light;
> Protect us by Thy might,
> Great God, our King.

Complete front view of Old Fort Mackinac.

U. S. ARMY OFFICERS SERVING AT FORT MACKINAC

From 1796 to 1895.

(Note—The author has endeavored to gather the names of officers from the War department records. Their rank is given as recorded upon their assignment to duty at the Island fort. In nearly all cases promotions later followed. Frequently names appear again and again in the roster through successive years, as is the case with Lieut. Col. John R. Bailey, Asst. Surgeon, whose service at Fort Mackinac extended to nearly a half century. In the following list names appear only once, at the date of fort duty assignment in the records. On file at the State Park office are more complete records of re-assignments to duty here, and these records will gladly be shown to descendants or relatives of army officers, or inquiries by mail cheerfully answered so far as possible from the information at hand).

1796—Major Henry Burback.

      Lieut. Ebenezer Massey.

      Capt. Abner Prior.

      Lieut. John Michael.

1800—Lieut. John Wiley.

1802—Major Thomas Hunt.

      Capt. Josiah Dunham.

      Surgeon's Mate Francis LeBarron.

1804—Lieut. Colonel Jacob Kingsbury.

1807—Lieut. Jonathan Eastman.

1808—Capt. Lewis Howard (Died Jan. 18, 1811).

      Lieut. Porter Hanks.

      Lieut. Archibald Darragh.

Surgeon's Mate Sylvester Day. (Captured
by the British July 17th, 1812, and held by
them until turned over by Col. Robert Mc-
Douall to Colonel Anthony Butler, U. S.
Army, on July 18th, 1815, at the conclusion of the War of 1812, won by the Americans.)

1815—Colonel Anthony Butler.
  Capt. Willoughby Morgan.
  Major Talbot Chambers.
  Capt. Joseph Kean.
  Capt. John O'Fallow.
  Lieut. John Heddelson.
  Lieut. John S. Gray.
  Lieut. William Armstrong.
  Capt. Benjamin Pierce.
  Lieut. Robert McCallum.
  Lieut. George S. Wilkins.
  Lieut. John S. Pierce.
  Lieut. John S. Baird.

1816—Colonel John Miller.
  Major John McNeil.
  Major Charles Gratiot.
  Capt. William Whistler.
  Capt. John Greene.
  Lieut. Daniel Curtis.
  Lieut. John Garland.
  Lieut. Turly F. Thomas.
  Lieut. Henry J. Conway.
  Lieut. James Dean.
  Lieut. Andrew Lewis.
    Paymaster Asher Phillips.

1817—Lieut. William S. Evelith.

1818—Lieut. Edward Brooks.
      Post Surgeon Joseph P. Russel.
1819—Lieut. Joseph Gleason.
      Lieut. Col. William Lawrence.
      Lieut. Peter T. January.
      Lieut. John Peacock.
1821—Post Surgeon William Beaumont.
      Capt. Thomas C. Legate.
      Lieut. Elijah Lyon.
      Lieut. James A. Chambers.
      Lieut. Joshua Barney.
1822—Lieut. James M. Spencer.
1823—Capt. A. C. W. Fanning.
      Lieut. Samuel W. Hunt.
      Lieut. Aaron H. Wright.
      Lieut. George H. Crosman.
      Lieut. Stewart Cowan.
1825—Capt. William Hoffman.
      Asst. Surgeon Richard S. Satterlee.
      Lieut. Carlos A. Wait.
      Lieut. Seth Johnson.
1826—Capt. Alexander B. Thompson.
      Lieut. David Brooks.
1827—Lieut. James G. Allen.
      Asst. Surgeon Edwin James.
      Lieut. Ephraim K. Barnum.
      Lieut. Edwin V. Sumner.
      Lieut. Samuel T. Heintzelman.
1828—Capt. Sullivan Burbank.
      Capt. Robert McCabe.
      Lieut. Charles F. Morton.
      Lieut. William Alexander.

Major Josiah H. Vose.

Lieut. Abner B. Hetzel.

1829—Lieut. Enos Cutler.

Lieut. James Engle.

Lieut. Amos Foster.

Lieut. Moses E. Merrill.

Lieut. Ephraim Kirby Smith.

Lieut. Isaac Lynde.

Lieut. Caleb C. Sibley.

Lieut. William E. Cruger.

Lieut. Louis T. Jamison.

1830—Lieut. Henry Clark.

1831—Lieut. John T. Collingworth.

Asst. Surgeon Robert McMillan.

1832—Col. George M. Brooks.

Capt. Waddy V. Cobbs.

Lieut. Joseph S. Gallagher.

Lieut. George W. Patten.

Lieut. Thomas Stockton.

Captain B. F. Russell.

1833—Lieut. Joseph R. Smith.

Lieut. James W. Penrose.

Asst. Surgeon Charles S. Frailey.

Asst. Surgeon George F. Turner.

1834—Captain John Clitz.

Lieut. Jesse H. Leavenworth.

1835—Lieut. James V. Bomford.

Lieut. J. B. Kingsbury.

Lieut. Messana R. Patrick.

1836—Lieut. James W. Anderson.

Asst. Surgeon Erastus B. Wolcott.

1839—Capt. Samuel McKenzie.

Lieut. Arnold Elzey Jones.

1840—Captain Harvey Brown.
Lieut. John W. Phelps.
Lieut. John C. Pemberton.
1841—Capt. Patrick H. Galt.
Capt. Alexander Johnston.
Lieut. George C. Thomas.
Lieut. George W. Getty.
Lieut. William Chapman.
Lieut. Spencer Norvell.
Lieut. Henry Whiting.
Lieut. John M. Jones.
Asst. Surgeon Henry Holt.
1842—Capt. Martin Scott.
Chaplain Rev. John O'Brien.
1843—Capt. Moses E. Merrill.
Lieut. William Root.
Lieut. John C. Robinson.
Asst. Surgeon Levi H. Holden.
1844—Asst. Surgeon John Byrne.
1845—Capt. Silas Casey.
Lieut. George C. Westcott.
Lieut. Joseph P. Smith.
Lieut. Fred Steele.
Asst. Surgeon Charles C. Keeney.
1847—Capt. Frazey M. Winans.
Capt. Morgan L. Gage.
Lieut. Michael P. Doyle.
Lieut. Caleb F. Davis.
Lieut. William F. Chittenden.
1848—Capt. Charles H. Larned.
Lieut. Hiram Dryer.
Lieut. William N. B. Beall.
1849—Lieut. Joseph L. Tidball.
Asst. Surgeon Joseph B. Brown.

1850—Asst. Surgeon Charles H. Laub.

1851—Lieut. David L. Russel.

1852—Capt. Joseph H. Bailey.
Capt. Thomas Williams.
Lieut. George W. Rains.
Lieut. Jacob Culbertson.

1854—Asst. Acting Surgeon John R. Bailey.

1855—Lieut. John H. Greland.

1856—Lieut. Edward F. Bagley.
Lieut. William R. Terrell.
Lieut. Joseph H. Wheelock.

1857—Lieut. Henry Benson.
Lieut. Guilford D. Bailey.

1858—Capt. John F. Head.
Capt. Henry C. Pratt.
Lieut. Henry A. Smalley.

1859—Capt. William A. Hammond.
Lieut. George R. Hartsuff.

1860—Capt. George E. Cooper.

1862—Capt. Grover C. Wormer.
Lieut. Elias F. Sutton.
Lieut. Louis Hertmeyer.
Asst. Surgeon John Gregg.
Asst. Surgeon Charles W. LaBoutillier.
Chaplain James Knox.

1866—Capt. Jerry N. Hill.
Lieut. Washington L. Wood.

1867—Captain John Mitchell Reed.
Lieut. Edwin C. Gaskill.
Lieut. Julius Stommell.
Asst. Surgeon Hiram R. Mills.

1869—Captain Leslie Smith.
Lieut. John Leonard.

Lieut. Matthew Markland.

1870—Capt. Samuel S. Jessop.

1871—Lieut. Thomas Sharp.

1872—Capt. William N. Notson.

1873—Capt. Carlos Carvallo, Asst. Surgeon.

1874—Capt. Carlos J. Dickey.

Lieut. John McA. Webster.

Capt. J. Victor De Hanne.

Lieut. W. W. Dougherty.

1875—Major Alfred L. Hough.

1876—Capt. Joseph Bush.

Lieut. Thomas H. Fisher.

Lieut. Fielding L. Davis.

1877—Major Charles A. Webb.

Capt. Peter Moffatt, Asst. Surgeon.

Lieut. John G. Ballance.

Lieut. Theodore Mosher, Jr.,

1878—Lieut. Oscar D. Ladley.

1879—Major Edwin E. Sellers.

Capt. Charles L. Davis.

Lieut. Dwight H. Kelton.

Lieut. Walter T. Duggan.

Lieut. Bogardus Eldridge.

Lieut. Edward H. Plummer.

1880—Capt. George W. Adair, Asst. Surgeon.

1882—Capt. William H. Corbusier, Asst. Surgeon.

1883—Lieut. John Adams Perry.

1884—Lieut. Col. George K. Brady.

Capt. Greenleaf A. Goodale.

Lieut. Edward B. Pratt.

Lieut. Stephen O'Connor.

Lieut. Benjamin C. Morse.

Lieut. Calvin S. Cowles.

Lieut. J. Rozier Clagett.

1886—Capt. William C. Manning.

Lieut. George B. Davis.

1887—Lieut. Charles E. Woodruff, Asst. Surgeon.

1889—Asst. Surgeon Harlan E. McVay.

1890—Capt. Jacob H. Smith.

Major Edwin M. Coates.

Capt. Charles T. Witherell.

Lieut. Edmund D. Smith.

Lieut. Zebulon B. Vance, Jr.

Lieut. Woodridge Geary.

Lieut. Henry G. Learnard.

1891—Capt. Alexander McGuard.

Lieut. Joseph Frazier.

1892—Capt. Edwin F. Gardner, Asst. Surgeon.

1893—Lieut. John Howard.

Lieut. James Ronayne.

1894—Major Clarence E. Bennett.

1895—Lieut. Woodridge Geary.

Lieut. E. M. Johnson, Jr.

Sally port entrance to Fort Mackinac.

LIST OF ILLUSTRATIONS

Page

Old Fort Mackinac...........................Frontispiece

The landing of Nicolet on Mackinac Island, in June,
1634 10

Original French design of Fort Michilimackinac at St.
Ignace, 1762... 15

Typical picture of early forts at St. Ignace, Mackinaw
City and Sault Ste. Marie........................... 20

Death of Father Marquette, 1675...................... 25

Indians and LaSalle's "Griffin"...................... 30

Schneider's working model for reconstruction of Old
Fort Michilimackinac at Mackinaw City............ 45

Airplane view of restored Fort Michilimackinac at
Mackinaw City 58

Indian Tepee inside restored fort at Mackinaw City.... 72

Preparing the "pipe of peace"........................ 84

Entrance to Michilimackinac State Park at Mackinaw
City, Michigan...................................... 99

Airplane view of Fort Mackinac today.................107

South view, Old Fort Mackinac and Marquette Statue 115

Sentry duty at Fort Mackinac, 1870...................122

Major Andrew Hunter Holmes..........................130

Officers' stone quarters, Fort Mackinac...............138

Dress parade at the old fort, 1852.....................146

The John Jacob Astor House, Mackinac Island, 1833 ...154

Ancient Fort Holmes as accurately restored in 1936 on
the hill overlooking Fort Mackinac.................162

Eagle Scout Honor Guard barracks on Fort Mackinac
parade grounds.....................................170

Plan of buildings on Fort Mackinac...................175

Complete front view of Old Fort Mackinac............180

Sally port entrance to Fort Mackinac..................189